# Seasons of Love

# Seasons of Love

ASHLEY WILLIAMS

*To my Uncle Jay*
*One of my first experiences of unconditional love, despite*
*any shortcomings I have always loved you and always will.*
*Always thinking of you and missing you. You would be so*
*proud if you could see me now!*

# Contents

# CHAPTER 1

# The Beginning

Everything always seems right in the beginning. The start of things can be so refreshing. A new start brings endless possibilities. A new relationship feels so good, and one may think that nothing can go wrong in the beginning. It's like when a baby is first born, they come into this world, and the beginning of their life starts. They are cherished by so many loved ones, their mother and father can't seem to put them down. Every cry or whimper is answered with eagerness. They are treated with love and their every need is taken care of. All they know is that they are somewhere new, that they have never experienced before. At least not that their ego can remember at this point. But this is only the beginning, this baby has no idea of what they just entered into. Because in the beginning everything is nice and so refreshing, but it does not stay that way. As the baby grows, they soon realize that their newness wears off and things begin to change. The baby grows into a toddler, moves on into those grade school years, and later becomes an adult. The baby will experience so much as the beginning turns into this ongoing process. The baby will have their first fall, they will notice that their cries do not produce the same reactions from their mom and dad. That newness wears off and the baby is now in a world that can be cold, experiencing the unexpected. As the baby grows into a child and later an adult, the realization that life can be full of twists and turns becomes apparent. The beginning is no longer and that feeling is gone. It can be very similar in a relationship. Boy meets girl and sparks fly, there seems to be endless love, and nothing can go wrong. As the two get to know each other, they begin to realize that lots can go wrong, and that love is not so endless after all. Love can be such a powerful word, such a meaningful experience. One that should be felt by all people who walk this earth with no exception. Love does not have to be hard, yet we make it extremely hard when we see fit. Instead of giving love freely, we hold on to it, afraid to let it go thinking that it can end in disaster. Unfortunately, many times it does, a woman may give her love away and find out that it was not appreciated by the recipient. A man may decide that he is in love with his mate, but that love is given to another with no regard for her. Love can be hard, although it shouldn't be. But in the beginning, love is wonderful, it never seems that the special feeling that love brings will ever go away. I can still remember the first time that I ever met my husband. I remember the beginning like it was yesterday. I remember the first time I experienced love with him and how it felt so good and refreshing. I could never imagine the roller coaster that I would experience with this man. The beginning did not tell me this, it just provided me with that wonderful feeling that I thought would never end. I met my husband in high school, we had French class together. Honestly, the first time I met him I was not impressed, and you could say that I really did not like him. His energy was not good and he was mean to one of my favorite teachers. I never imagined that I would fall in love with him many times throughout my life. It was summertime and I was 14 years old, I saw him coming up the street. He saw me and from that day everything changed. We were young and he smelled so good, from there we were a couple. He liked me and I liked him- all of a sudden and that was all she wrote. That summer turned into years of life spent with an individual that was my everything and love as I knew it. It was also full of a lot of drama, hurt, and pain that I could never imagine. Over 20 years of on-again and off-again, I love you today, tomorrow I hate you. At the end, we would finally go our separate ways and I would be left in pieces. Feeling as if I could not breathe and that life was over as I knew it. I was a mess; this is my journey in my own words. Hopefully, these words will help someone who experienced love in a way that it is not. Someone who was in a similar spot as I was, feeling as if they could not move on without a particular person or thing in their life. I am here to tell you that you can go on, and I know this because I was there. I had that feeling that my life was over, I lost the love of my life, and I would not be able to move on. I felt that pain, and although I would never be the same, I was able to move on. I am hoping that my journey will help someone who is in a bad space to get up and change their circumstances. Love does not hurt, and it is not messy, it will not fail you. We must tell ourselves this and remember to love ourselves so that we can provide love to others. We must also love ourselves so that we can realize how love works and know the difference between love and what we think is love. Through my journey, I have learned to love myself. I have a clear idea of what love is and what it is not. I was not aware of this in the beginning, I thought love was everything that it was not. So, I am grateful for my journey, the good and the bad because it made me who I am today. Without this experience of what love is not, I would have never discovered what love is. So back to the story, the beginning, when everything felt so right and no wrong could even be imagined. We were young and in love, my boyfriend and I, and it was us against the world. I loved him and he loved me, and we would be together forever. The only thing is that forever is not a lifetime, forever is as long as its suitable. So, my boyfriend, who later became my husband, was the love of my life. At a very young age, he came into my life, and I loved him with all my heart and everything I had. I met him when I was 14 years old, and by the time I was 16 years old and 11 months, I was having his baby. We spent two years together, as boyfriend and girlfriend, claiming love and doing things that only adults should be doing. It resulted in us being teenage parents, giving birth to a 6-pound and 5-ounce baby girl. She added to our love and would be the glue that kept us together for many years. We were both determined to provide our baby with love and to be the best parents that we could be. In the beginning, we did good but as we know the beginning is always good. I soon learned that raising a child would not be easy and it was definitely not how I imagined that it would be with the love of my life. I had plans for my family, but my boyfriend was not on the same page and those plans soon went straight out the window. Our baby girl was born in 2001 and my boyfriend did his first bid in prison before our daughter turned 1 year old. Although I was a teenage mom, I had plans to go to school with the support of my man. He would take care of me and our baby while I prepared to put us in a better spot for our future. I would finish school and get a good job, and then my man would learn a trade or go to school, while I supported the family. It was simple and my plan was fool proof, there was no way we could fail. It's funny because I can't recall the season, but I know that before my baby was six months old, I was suddenly alone, without my man. It was the first time he left me, but it would not be the last. For the next four to five years, my man and I would take our first ride on the roller coaster of life. I would finish high school, while he was incarcerated, which meant going to the prom without him. Raising our child alone and working a part-time job while writing him and looking forward to phone calls. My child's father was released from prison halfway, where my child who was now a little over one year old and I would visit on a weekly basis. Our baby had forgotten who her father was and at first, she gave him a very hard time. He would pick her up and she would fuss and fight, but things got better. We made it through the storm, and we were back together again. Now I was a high school graduate planning to attend college while working at the hospital. Our child was growing up to be a smart little girl- talking, walking and potty trained. My man was home and life was good, we were together and preparing for the future. Although I was still young, I was determined to be a good mother and a good girlfriend and to get my life together. I would complete one year of college before dropping out to work full-time. It seemed like the smart thing to do at the time, after all, I had a child to take care and college seemed to be senseless and a waste of time. Later in life, I would regret this decision but at the time money and raising my daughter were a priority. My man, although I loved him, was not too dependable even when he was out of jail. He did what he wanted when he wanted and that did not always benefit me and my daughter. Now that I look back on this time, I am pretty sure that my man messed around with other women. I would hear rumors once in a blue, that he had slept with a girl on a drunken night. He was living a different life, in the streets, drinking, smoking, gambling and selling drugs. At the moment I thought that myself and our daughter were his priority but that may not have been the case. We did family things, such as spending time together, we even stayed over at each other's house despite continuing to live with our mothers. But my man was in the streets and that is where he placed all his love. He would be home for a little over a year before returning back to jail. Right before he caught his charge that would land him another 18 months in prison, I discovered that he was messing around with one of his old flings from middle school. This girl had his heart as a child, and he had decided that he wanted her again as an adult. My man had stopped talking to me, he was acting differently toward me all of a sudden. But I didn't realize that it was due to another woman until one day I pulled up to pick my daughter up and witnessed it with my own eyes. My man was outside with our daughter and another woman and her children playing. It broke my heart, and I instantly knew by their body language that something was going on. She was the reason that his behavior had suddenly changed. I would spend months trying to keep tabs on him with the help of his sisters, who at this point I had close relations with. I was running down behind this man who no longer wanted to be with me. I tried to use our daughter as bait to get him back. Nothing worked, I would call him, cuss him out and hang up. Just to call him back, beg and cry for him to stop acting like this. Nothing worked, finally one day I was fed up and I decided that I was going to take action. I was not going to just sit here and allow some woman to take my man. So I grabbed my daughter and walked up the street to this woman's house. It just so happened she lived a few houses down from my daughter's great-grandmother. I dropped my daughter off at her aunt, my man's oldest sister, and walked up the three flights of stairs to this woman's house. I was going to confront her and ask her if she was messing with my man. I already knew the answer, I may have even expected him to be in the house with her. But I did not care, I was emotional and I had enough, someone was going to give me answers and deal with my feelings today. I knocked on the door and she answered, it seemed as if she was expecting me. She didn't invite me in, but she definitely admitted to messing with him. After hearing this, I made one request and that was to come outside because we are going to fight. She refused so I kindly stepped into her house and begin to pound on her. I did not come there to talk, and I was not living until I took my anger out on someone. In my mind, this woman was wrong, she had broken up my family and she had to pay. We fought in her kitchen, in front of her daughter and I did not care. My man's sister finally came upstairs and broke us up and walked me down the stairs. At this point, I was still livid, not one emotion had left with any of the blows to this woman's face. I was hurt, I was crying, and I had very little control over myself. Things had ended bad, and I had no idea how I would move on from this. Of course, on this day, my man would choose to go with his new girlfriend. And I went home, I had won the physical fight, but my heart was broken and there was no relief. I was alone and I wanted everyone to feel the pain I felt. Days went by and I am not even sure how we started talking again. Most likely our daughter played a part in rekindling our relationship. But however, it happened, we were back together, and my man was on his way back to prison. We spent the last few months of his freedom together as a family. I vowed to be there for him during this tough time and I planned to wait for my man while he was in prison. Once again, he was doing a bid in prison, and I was doing it with him. Despite the fact that a few short months ago, he didn't want anything to do with me, I loved him, and I knew deep down he loved me also. So, for almost two years, I kept money on his books, made frequent visits with our child, and looked forward to the calls. I don't know what it was, but I really loved this man, and I was determined to show him how much. Anybody that has had a relationship with an individual in prison knows just how smoothly it can go on their part. They will tell you everything you want to hear, make all these promises and everything is good. Afterall the individual is in a structured setting with lots of time to think and basically do nothing but pass the time. And the loved ones outside just want the individual home and choose to believe any and everything that comes out of their mouth. Doing the bid with my man was exhausting but we made it and he came home. At this point, our child would be entering kindergarten next fall. I was so happy to have my man home and hoped that things would go right. I was working and taking caring of things and really had no expectations of him. I just wanted my family together and for everything to be okay. My man and I had been through a lot, break ups and heartbreaks, along with being separated by prison walls. It was a lot and many times, it almost felt as if I would not make it. Love kept us together and now that my man was finally home, we could finally start living again. Life was good, we were happy, and things were going well. My man did slowly get back into the streets but that was fine. He would remain focused this time and prioritize me and our daughter- at least that was what I thought. Before our daughter made it to kindergarten, my man would be back in jail. He would be facing time for something a little more serious than selling drugs. I was scared and fed up, I was not going to be able to continue to live life like this. I will never forget the last night we spent together. It was at my man's house; he was still living with his mother. We had decided to stay there and leave our daughter with my mother. That night was stressful because we both had a lot on our minds. My man had just been involved in a serious crime and we did not know what the outcome would be. I don't even know how we managed to fall asleep that night, but we were awakened in the middle of the night with flashlights and police officers in our faces. They had come for him in the middle of the night, and he would be taken from me once again. This was the first time, that my man would suddenly be leaving. Previously, we would go to court many times and his exit was some-what planned. But not that night, this was a little more serious and within minutes the police snatched my man up and put him in the back of a police car. I thought he would be gone forever, and I was scared. He left that night and would not return home anytime soon. There was no bounding him out, he would remain in jail until his trial was over and he received his sentence. We were in our early twenties and this was not how I envisioned life for my family. Once again, my man had let me down, the streets received his love, and I got the little he had left. I remember going to visit my man shortly after the night that he was picked up. I was sad and upset and I let it show. I was tired of faking it and decided it was time for me to express my feelings. I demanded that my man put me and our child first this time around. He could do this by taking the stand and confessing to the crime he witnessed. This is also known as snitching and anyone who is in the streets knows this is a huge no-no. Of course my man was not trying to hear this shit and probably couldn't even understand why I was bringing this up. He shot me down and let me know firmly that he would not be discussing anything about that night with anyone from the law. He would have to sit in prison, once again and would do so with no regard for his family. He was choosing the streets as he always did because this is what was best for him. Up until now, I didn't realize how much my man really loved the streets and seemingly felt more obligated to it than to myself and our daughter. Now I knew where he stood, I realized that this would be our life if I decided to stay. He would always come home and return to the streets and that came with a lot of bull-shit. I did not want to do this anymore and I would not do it. I took it extremely personally that my man would rather sit in jail instead of coming home and being with his family. So, for this bid, I would not be there with him. That visit would be the last visit that I would make to see him. We would go years without seeing one another and needless to say we grew apart. The phone calls were far and in between and eventually stopped completely. I left the prison that day and suddenly I had a change of heart.

I was moving on and living life for me and my daughter. I was single and had no love for my man who was now my ex. I had loved him for so long, but the love ran out. I did not have the energy to fight against the feelings, so I moved on. I moved on by going out to the bars and the clubs. I moved on by messing with multiple men and refusing to give my heart to anyone. Life was all about me at this point. I went to work, I played mommy, and I went out and had fun. I was drinking and smoking and having a lot of fun. My ex and I grew distant, he would be in prison for a couple of years, and I no longer cared. I partied a lot, but I also took care of business for myself and my child. I had a good job and moved into my own apartment. For the first time since I had been with my man, I finally accepted that we would not be together forever. This was the start of my new life, and it did not include him. I had even started to date another man exclusively and it felt good. I didn't have to complete with the streets with my new man because he wasn't that type of guy. When my ex came home from this bid, I did not welcome him. There was no celebration, and I had no feelings for him. We had grown apart and were at two different points in our life. My ex and I would spend many years fighting over our daughter and simply not getting along. I think I even hated him, and I would express this as often as I could. My love had turned to hate, and I no longer wanted to share our child. I made things very hard for him when it came to her, and we had a very rocky relationship for many years. We both moved on, I had a new boyfriend whom I was living with, and my ex was involved with whomever and living his life. We had gotten over one another and eventually, communication would get a little easier. Our daughter got older, and life went on without us being together. Time would go by; my ex continued to be in and out of jail. I got pregnant with my youngest daughter and ended a 5-year relationship with her father about one year after she was born. I found myself single with two children, but I was focused and happy. I was in a different place mentally and emotionally. A lot had taken place since my first child was born, I had grown up and had life experiences to reflect on. My ex was always present in our child's life, he would not have it any other way. Regardless of the hard time that I gave him, he developed a strong and healthy relationship with his daughter. As I mentioned earlier, she played a huge part in our relationship and she is the reason that we found ourselves back together after spending many years apart. It was the summer of 2012, my daughter made a special request, she wanted to spend her birthday with both of her parents. The timing was everything, I was single, and my ex was not currently involved with anyone. We were also communicating effectively and getting along well. So, we decided to grant our daughter's request and spend her birthday together at *Six flags*. This one day would turn into eight years of love, pain, suffering, marriage, cheating and divorce. This one day would lead to my spiritual growth and lead me to the person that I am today. Today I know love unconditionally, today I can let things go instead of holding on to the past. Today I understand that there is nothing on this earth that is worth holding onto. I understand that God loves us all regardless of our mistakes and if God can let them go, so should we. Today I choose to be happy and to move in love. That day at *Six Flags* my ex and I got on our second roller coaster ride of life. We would spend another eight years together and it would be a bumpy ass ride for the both of us. The last eight years had been full of a lot of ups and downs, yet it had allowed me to develop and become a genuine person who knows how to love regardless of the circumstance. These last eight years had allowed me to experience what love is not so that today I know what love is. In 2012, my ex and I decided to start a new beginning after all that we had gone through. Something happened at *Six Flags* in which we both realized that love still exists amongst us. We decided to give love another try; I had no idea what I was getting myself into. This is my story.

# CHAPTER 2

# The Affair

My man, who turned into an ex, became my man again and eventually my husband. We got married on October 7, 2017, five years, and two months after spending that day at *Six Flags* with our daughter. A lot had happened in those five years since our day at Six Flags. By the time I got back together with my ex, I had a 3-year-old daughter, and my ex had a baby on the way. Basically, I was setting myself up for more bullshit. Now that I look back on it, I am not sure why I decided to go back to this man. During the years that we spent apart, I vowed never to be with him again. Maybe I was lonely, being that I was single when we went to *Six Flags*. In that short time that we spent together, it just felt so comfortable, and we did not part from that day on. I stuck it out with him, with his baby on the way with another woman. It was hard watching him have this baby with another woman, but I had made the decision to be with him regardless of the situation. Not only did he have a newborn baby, but my ex also had a drinking and drug problem that I was not aware of. What seemed like new beginnings quickly turned into a lot of nonsense that I could have gone without. But I committed myself to the relationship despite some red flags that should have led to an early departure. I really could have saved myself from a lot of pain, stress, and unnecessary loss if I would have paid closer attention when we got back together. Before we got married, my ex who is now my new man cheated on me with his child's mother and other women. He took my car when he wanted to, leaving me to figure out how to get back and forth to work. He was drinking, smoking and doing whatever else he chose, while I sat at home worried about him. I would call him, and he would not answer and not come home all night. All this took place the first year that we got back together. Things were worse now than when we were younger, yet I stayed. Then my man went back to jail, leaving his daughter and me back in that familiar spot. This time he would do a little more than three years in jail. Although when he went in, we were not doing the best, I decided to stick with him. For some reason, I had these strong emotions for him, and I wanted to prove my love to him. I made frequent visits, made sure money was on his books and that he was able to call multiple times a week. I did not cheat on him; I did not even look at other men for three years. I was fully committed, working two and three jobs, while going to school to take care of my family. The three years apart were hard, but we made it work the best we could. My man made me a promise that he was going to come home and do better. We had plans to live a nice and normal life from here on out. I just knew that everything was going to be alright. How could it not, after all, I did just put my life on hold for this man. He must have known and understood the depth of my love after this, there was no way we could go wrong. These were my thoughts, I truly thought we would finally be happy and get things right once my man got home. In 2016, he made it to the halfway house and the excitement that I felt was indescribable. It was like a dream come true, to be able to see him and touch him outside of prison walls. And honestly, after 3 years of no affection or sex, I was more than ready to spend some alone time with my man. We started things off right, and everything seemed good. He got a job; I was working two jobs while working towards my bachelor's degree. The kids were happy, and life was good. But with me and my man's track record, the good never lasted. I remember our first fight after he came home, he had been home for about three months. I had started to notice that he was acting strange with his cell phone and one day a thought just popped into my head that my man was acting strange. Shortly after that thought, I worked up the nerve to ask him to let me see his phone. Well, that was the wrong thing to ask, because he got very defensive and it led to a huge fight. He was not trying to let me see his phone as if he had something to hide (which I would later find out that he had a lot to hide). So, we had our first fight due to his strange behavior and my suspicions. But we were able to move on from it and decided that we wanted to buy a house. How we went from fighting over his suspicious behavior to buying a house together, I cannot explain. One afternoon, I ran the idea by him that I wanted to buy a house and that I wanted to do it with his help. We talked about it and he agreed that it was a good idea. From there we decided that we would start the process of buying a house. Over the next six months, things were pretty smooth for us. I did notice that my man had started to drink again, but he was also working and seemed to be focused on our relationship and family. I let the whole phone thing go and it seemed as if my man and I were in a good place. I got approved for a loan to buy a house and we begin house-hunting. House-hunting was fun and finally we were able to pick out a nice house that was suitable for our family. We moved into our new home in June 2017 and it felt great. We were teenage parents, had been through many ups and down and we had finally accomplished something. We became homeowners and it was a really good feeling. We were on a high but it would not last. Within the first six weeks of moving into our new home, I got a bomb dropped on me. Our daughter noticed that her dad was texting a woman while we were all driving in the car one night. She was in the back seat and had a full view of the messages that he was receiving and sending. She also managed to get his pass code to his cell phone. My daughter came to me the next day and let me know that her dad was texting with another woman and it did not look good. She also gave me his passcode and suggested that I look at his phone. I can't even explain how it felt to be told by our daughter that something was going on which involved another woman. Of course, this would not be the first time my man had cheated on me, but it was so unexpected. Coming from our child only added to the negative feelings. I took her suggestion and got my hands on that phone when the opportunity presented itself. My man was outside in the yard with his best friend and his best friend's girlfriend. The phone was sitting on the nightstand on the charger. My heart began to pound as I snatched it off the nightstand and entered the passcode. My life changed forever after this day and it would never be the same. That day I discovered that my man was cheating once again with some woman. The messages went on for months and months. It was devasting. At this point, my hands were shaking and I felt like my heart was going to beat out of my chest. I can still remember the day as if it were yesterday. Such a horrible feeling and I did not know what to do next. I did not that my suspicious from a few months earlier were real. My man had a lot to hide and that is why he became so defensive when I asked about his phone that morning. After going through his phone, I begin to pace back and forth in our family room. I was trying to think of my next action, but I could not think straight. I wanted to stay in control of my feelings, but I had already unraveled and there was no coming back. All I felt was hurt and pain, I wanted an explanation from this man. As if an explanation would take the pain away and fix the situation. After what felt like an hour, but was really just a few minutes, I decided I was going to confront him about the findings in his phone. I don't remember how, but somehow, I got him into our bedroom, and I confronted him. I can't remember exactly what I said, but I remember that I was crying and shaking. He instantly started with the lies, he actually confessed to cheating on me and said that it had started a few weeks. He expressed regret and said sorry repeatedly. We sat in that room for some time and his friend eventually left without any goodbyes. At a time in which we should have been celebrating our accomplishments, my man had just confessed to cheating on me. And the proof was there, I saw the texts with my own eyes. They were constantly communicating with one another; pictures were sent, and it was clear that they were involved with one another. At this moment I had to accept that my man had picked up where he left off before going to prison three years ago. After all that I had done to show him how much I loved him, he came home and begin cheating on me again. He had promised that things would be different when he was in prison and I believed him. We just brought a house, which he agreed to do with me. The whole time he was talking to another woman, telling her a completely different story. All I felt was pain, all I could do was cry and just wonder why this was happening. That night, my man told me he would stop communicating with her. I don't even know if I believed him. I was completely numb. The next few days were a blur and I walked around very quietly, consumed in my thoughts. I had planned a family vacation before I discovered the text message. We decided to go despite the issues that we were having. This would be a time to spend together with the kids and to reset. I guess I was going to try to work this out. After all, there was no way I was letting this woman come in here and have my man. He loved me; he didn't love her so she would have to let this little thing they had gone. We go on vacation, and it was completely horrible. My man and I fought every night beginning with the first night. He was asleep on the couch in the waterfront condo that we had rented. His phone was right there in clear view, and I could not resist going in it. I should have just left the phone on the table because I was not prepared for what I found. This man was still communicating with this woman and had even informed her about our recent discussion about their relationship. He was continuing to play games and had not stopped the communicating with her as he promised. This time there were no tears, I was pissed, and I reacted. I took her number and decided to text her and let her know the truth. I let her know that she was messing with my man and that she needed to stop. Her response was for me to enjoy my little family vacation. I wanted to come through the phone on this woman's ass, she had a lot of balls. I woke my man up and cussed his ass out about this woman. I don't even think he engaged with me about the matter, pointing out that we were on vacation with the kids, and this was not the time. I did not care, I demanded that he call this woman in front of me and tell her the truth. After ranting and raving for almost an hour, he called her and left her a voice message. I was satisfied until I discovered that he also sent her a text message trying to explain the message and asking this woman to be patient with him. Clearly, my man was playing both sides of the fence and this was only the beginning. The vacation was horrible, it began with fighting, and it ended with fighting. On the very last day, my man brought up marriage to me. I don't know what the hell he was thinking, and I was a damn fool to even entertain his suggestion. He suggested that we get married and promised that this woman did not mean anything to him. He took it upon himself to look up the requirements to get a marriage license and we set a date. Looking back on it, I don't know what I was thinking, this man was cheating on me and telling lots of lies to two women. Yet I was about to marry him, with the thought that he loved me and did not love her. I agreed to marry him on our last day of vacation. I wasn't excited about it, but I was hoping that his suggestion to get married meant that I was more important and that he loved me. I was hoping that he would stop all communications with this woman and that we could be happy, living our nice simple life as planned. About two months after the worse vacation that

I had ever experienced, our wedding date was here. A few weeks after we returned home from vacation, my man continued to press the issue of marriage. It seemed like this is what he really wanted and that brought me some relief. So, I went with it, we planned to marry as soon as possible and made it happen on October 7th, 2017. My wedding day was uneventful and I had second thoughts the entire time. A few weeks before our wedding, I had a conversation with my man and expressed to him my expectations of him as my husband. I told him that I was okay with the drinking, I was okay with making more money than him. I let him know that I loved him for him and would take him with his flaws and all. The one thing that I would not deal with was infidelity, I was not going to be in a love triangle with him and another woman. I asked him if he understood and if he could handle being my husband under these terms and he said yes. Leading up to our wedding, I would not check my man's cellphone, too afraid of what I might find. I tried to push the past few months out of my mind and to be happy. I kept telling myself that my man understood and agreed to this and that everything would be okay. I recently read a wonderful book, called *The Four Agreements*, by Don Miguel Ruiz. In the book, Ruiz explains that as humans we have the tendency to make assumptions about everything and that the problem with making assumptions is that we believe they are true (Ruiz, 1997). These words spoke volumes to me as I read them because I made so many assumptions regarding my relationship with this man. Regardless of the red flags that were clear and right in my face, I still assumed many things. These assumptions were my reality and I had made them my truths. Don Miguel Ruiz also points out in his book that making assumptions in our relationships is asking for problems (Ruiz, 1997). Well, I guess I wanted all the smoke so to speak because I assumed that this marriage was going to fix all the problems that my man and I were experiencing. I assumed that my love would change him. I assumed that because I was being genuine, I would get the same in return. I assumed that my man would be honest and honor our agreement, which was our marriage. I assumed that he loved me and that would lead to him doing right by me. I assumed that I was different and that I meant more to him than any other woman in his life. I assumed that because he asked me to marry him, he was willing to put in the work for a happy life. I assumed that because I let him know what I was expecting, and he agreed that everything would be okay. I assumed a lot and I was wrong about everything. I truly did not get anything that I expected from my marriage. I did not expect the hurt, and pain that was caused by my husband. I did not expect the lies and bullshit that he put me through. I did not think that when I married him, it would be a long two-and-a-half years. Two-and-a-half-years of my husband having an affair. I wish I could say that we got married and lived a nice and peaceful life. It would be nice to report that my marriage was full of love and happiness. But that is not the case because I signed a contract with someone who didn't intend to keep up his end of the bargain. I viewed marriage as an opportunity to love another person and to have a life partner. Someone to go through the rest of my life with and to always have my back. I went into the marriage willing to be the best wife I could be and to put in the necessary effort for a successful marriage. I don't think my husband had the same thing in mind. Maybe he didn't realize the seriousness of marriage or maybe he just did not care. Regardless of his reasoning or view of marriage, my husband did not honor his part in our agreement. He did not marry me with the intention of doing right by me and our family. For along time, I would tell myself that I should have known better, I should have never agreed to marry this man who I knew was messing around with another woman. But at the moment, I really felt that love would save us and allow us to move past the mess and get to the good part. Unfortunately, things did not improve once we got married. About one month after getting married, I finally came face to face with the woman that my husband was cheating with. I was working my part-time job at the hospital lab and my husband texted me that he would be going out with his cousin and brother to have a few drinks. I didn't think much of the message and responded with okay, see you later. When I got off work, I find my husband passed out in our bed. He had been drinking which was another issue and fell asleep. There was that damn cell phone right next to him, as he slept fully clothed. Of course, I could not resist, and I picked the phone up and begin to go through it. One month after getting married, my husband continued to communicate with the same woman that he promised me he would not. I read the text messages and realized that he had no plans with his family members. Instead, he was planning to go spend some time with this woman. The last text message was from her, asking if he was ready. But my husband had passed out from drinking too much and never replied to the text. He was most likely planning to be out of the house before I got off work, but the liquor he consumed ruined those plans. I woke him up, cussing and yelling about what I had found. He didn't respond, but he tried to get me to calm down and come to bed. I was not having it, and eventually I left the house to cool off. I didn't have anywhere to go, so I pulled over on the next street from our house. I decided to call my sister-in-law and talk with her to calm myself down. My husband attempted to call me and left me a few text messages asking me to come back home but I ignored him. I needed some space to clear my head and calm down a little. While sitting on the phone with my sister-in-law, I witness my husband walking down the street and at the same time an SUV sped down the street. My husband got in the SUV, and it sped off. With my sister-in-law on the phone, I started following the car. At first, they did not know I was following them. But at the first stop light, I pulled up to the side of them so that they could be aware that they had been caught. This was the first time that I saw my husband with another woman, a woman with whom he was having an affair. I went crazy and began to yell for them to pull over. Being that the woman would not pull over, I gave chase. I was not playing with this woman or my husband, my adrenaline was overflowing, and I was ready for anything. My goal was to get this woman to pull over, snatch her out of the car and whip her ass. She must have known that I had something for her because she was not pulling over. Or maybe it was my husband directing her to keep going. Whatever it was, it led to a high-speed chase on the highway. I was weaving in and out of traffic to keep up with them. I passed red lights and cut a few cars off as they honked their horns. I did not care; I was going to follow them until they pulled over. I called my husband repeatedly, but he kept sending me to voice mail. He even had the nerve to send me a text message demanding that I stop following them. I was not trying to hear that nonsense. Instead, I rammed my car into the back of the SUV and continued to chase them on the highway. The chase went on for about 30 minutes, this woman drove down route 8 south for about 12-13 exits. She got off at exit 14 and proceeded to get back on the high, driving in the opposite direction. I guess she was trying to shake me, but I was ready for it and continued to chase her, praying that no state troopers would be out this night and hoping that despite my gas light being on, I would not run out of gas. The whole time that I was chasing the SUV, my husband was plotting how to get his self out of this situation. Finally, he made her pull over and he got out of the car. He walked towards my car, got in and the SUV pulled off. I still wanted to chase the vehicle, keeping in mind my goal to beat this woman's ass. My husband did not allow it. Instead, he instructed me to pull over into the shopping plaza so we could talk. Sitting in the parking lot, I began to cry and ask him why. His response was that I was pushing him away and that I have no idea where this was coming from. We had been married for a little more than a month and up until tonight, there had been no issues. But my husband was manipulating me, something he did so well. He was trying to get the smoke off his self and place the blame on me. Like I had somehow pushed him into another woman's arms. This was the first time that I caught my husband cheating with his mistress. It would not be the last. We would spend our whole marriage in this ridiculous love triangle with the same woman. My husband would continue to cheat and manipulate me throughout our whole marriage. And I would continue to deal with it, causing myself lots of pain, sadness, and confusion. There would be many encounters with this woman and each time I would become irate. My anger would be towards the mistress first and then I would turn it towards my husband. The encounters started off with text messages and phone calls. I would cuss this woman out, every time I found text messages between her and my husband. She would respond by reminding me that she was sleeping with my husband and had no plans of stopping. The encounter went from calls and texting to face-to-face. My husband's mistress was crazy, she would sit outside my job and follow me home. One time, she followed my husband and me to our daughter's job. I will never forget seeing her face as we pulled over to drop our daughter off to work. As soon as I saw her, I hopped out of the car so fast. All I saw was red and I wanted to rip this woman's head off, how dare she follow us and show up at my daughter's job? Since she was following us, I felt she might as well get out of the car and confront me. But she wasn't that crazy, this woman rolled that car window up so fast as I approached. She ran her mouth from the car which was locked but she didn't dare step out of it. I was livid and attempted to get into the care of this woman but was pulled away by my husband. I couldn't take my anger out on her, so I took it out on my husband. He was the reason why we were in this situation, and he needed to know how I felt. There would be more situations like this, it seemed like every time, my husband and I were doing good, and I felt that the affair had finally ended, something would happen. I would go through his phone and find evidence that he was still communicating with her, or she would just pop up out of nowhere with her nonsense. As our marriage went on, the affair continued, and things got worse. My husband would leave our house for weeks at a time, not to return. I would call and message him, begging him to come home, but he would just ignore me. I would try to convince myself that he was staying with a friend or family member, but deep down I knew he was with her. It got to the point that even the good moments were stressful for me. Because I was always anticipating the negative. If he came back home and we were doing good, in the back of my mind, I would constantly be in fear of him leaving again. Each time we made up, my husband would promise to stop seeing his mistress, but I was always left disappointed. This woman was not going away, and neither was I, it also did not seem that my husband was going to make a decision. I went through a lot being married to my husband; his affair drained me and left me in pieces. I continued to stick with our marriage, hoping one day that he would stop messing around and be the husband that I needed him to be. I remained hopeful and I continued to pray to God to help our marriage. I told myself that I could love my husband through this mess. But nothing happened, we would have a few good months, but it would never last. My husband literally had an affair for our whole marriage. He allowed his mistress to get comfortable and disrespect me on several occasions. At one point, I begin to feel like the side chick, while she was the wife. In the end, he would leave me, and I finally made the decision that this would be the last time. I remember our last fight, my husband told me he was leaving and that I should just let him go. Those words stuck with me, and I finally began to understand that he did not want to be with me. I vowed to let him go because I loved him and because of that love I wanted him to be happy. Even if his happiness was not with me, I wanted my husband to be happy. I was so tired of fighting at that point, and it felt like my only option was to give up and let things go. I told myself that I would not allow this man to leave me ever again. The only way that I could ensure that this would be his last time leaving was to not allow him back in. I was done, my husband had put me through enough and I was no longer going to allow it. The affair was over because my husband no longer had a wife.

# CHAPTER 3

# I Need You

For the longest time, I thought that I could not live without my husband. He was my everything and life without him would not be the same. I would not have happiness without my man by my side. But honestly, I didn't have happiness with him by my side either. My marriage sucked and for me, the bad outweighed the good. I didn't realize this until after my husband and I split up and I begin to reflect on the years we spent together. I spent a lot of those years, alone because my man was in jail or simply choose not to come home. I shed a lot of tears and developed severe anxiety. Somehow, I had developed an attachment to my husband and truly felt that I needed him to breathe. Attachments are not healthy, and they can create a lot of issues for all parties involved. The person who develops the attachment may suffer if the individual they are attached to is not interested or disregards their feelings. The person who the attachment is for can also suffer because they may feel obligated to stick around or be with the attached despite other feelings. I honestly feel like my attachment to my husband had a negative impact on myself and my husband. Many times, I sat back and felt that I should have let him go a long time ago. The first time he left, I should have never asked him to come back. I was attached and there was no way that I was going to let him leave without a fight. If only I knew that being attached is not love and that my attachment would result in wasted time and energy. I am pretty sure that my attachment also impacted my husband in a negative way. Obviously, he was not ready to be a husband and he exhibited many signs, even before we got married. But I just could not let him go and each time he left; I would beg him to come back. It is possible that he felt obligated to me or just felt sorry for me. Either way, the relationship was not genuine on his part because each time he came home, it would not be long before he was caught cheating again. I needed him but he could not stop cheating, which led me to believe that he didn't love me. He didn't really want to be in this marriage, he just kept coming back for reasons other than love. All I knew was that I needed my husband and life would not be the same if he was not present with me. I cannot pinpoint when this happened, but it felt extremely scary to live life without him. How and why I developed such an attachment to this man, I will never be able to explain. I just really loved him with all my heart and once we got married, I could not imagine life without my husband. One of the main reasons I stayed in my marriage is that I was too afraid to face life alone. I really didn't think that it would be possible. I was not only attached to my husband, but I had also become dependent on him. I was dependent on him for my own happiness, and this was one of the worse things that I could do. David Hawkins points out in his book, *Letting Go*, that attachments and dependencies can make us feel weak and limited (Hawkins, 2012). I definitely felt like I was at a disadvantage in my marriage. I was not happy in my marriage because my husband would not do right, but I also did not have the strength to leave the situation. I can relate to David Hawkins' words because I lived them. I was attached and dependent, which led me to believe that I could not survive without my husband. It seemed as if I was in a lose-lose situation and trapped in a bubble of misery. A few times, I was told by family and friends that I was a strong woman, but I did not feel that strength. In the beginning, each time my husband cheated or left, I felt weaker and weaker. I would not eat or sleep when he disappeared. And when he came back home, I would suppress my feelings just to keep the peace. I was too afraid that I would push him away if I spoke up for myself and called him out. Those moments that I did speak up, always ended in an argument, he would even try to turn things around and blame me for his behavior. Most times when he came back home, I was just happy to have him around because I placed my happiness in his hands. I was looking outward instead of looking inward for my happiness. Happiness is another thing that is addressed by David Hawkins, he explains that an individual's source of happiness can be found from within. We should not search for happiness "out there", instead our happiness should be experienced as coming from within ourselves (Hawkins, 2012). If my happiness was from within, the things my husband did would have had less of an impact on me. When he cheated on me, I am sure it would still hurt but I would have had another source of happiness. The pain that he caused would have been less intense or I would have been better equipped to deal with it.

Through this process, I learned to search for happiness from within. We would all be happy if we just sought happiness from within. Material things do not matter, the people in our life will come and go. But we can still be happy if the happiness is within us as opposed to being in what we lost. A small child may receive a puppy for her fifth birthday. The puppy makes her happy and she becomes attached to it. But due to unfortunate circumstances, by the small child's next birthday, the puppy is removed from her life. That small child can choose to be sad for the rest of her life or she can choose to accept the circumstances and remain happy. The decision to remain happy is even easier if the child has a reservoir of happiness within herself. When we seek happiness from within, it allows us more control of our life and life circumstances. I placed my happiness in someone else's hands and that person had very little concern for my well-being. My husband came and went as he pleased, and he did what he wanted with no regard to my feelings. This led to me spending most of my marriage and life in general, unhappy. I needed and wanted my husband to be a good man and to love me. To prioritize me and our family, while keeping his end of our agreement. My husband was not only having an affair, but he was also inconsistent with helping with the bills. He would often spend his money on alcohol, drugs or gambling before giving me his share of the bill money. Our very first mortgage payment was late because he gambled his money away instead of having his share of the mortgage. I needed him to help with the bills, which he agreed to, but it did not take long for me to realize that my husband was not the dependable type. He fell short in many ways, but I continued to love him and the need for him to be a better man continued. It was very hard to accept that my husband was not the man that I needed him to be. For a very long time, I was in denial which only made things worse. I held on for a very long time, due to fear of the unknown. And when I look back on it, I wonder what it was that I was holding on to. My husband was cheating on me, lying to me and he came and went as he pleased and barely helped with the household. I was holding on to a dream that was really a nightmare. My husband was my norm, we had started dating back in high school. By the time we got married, he had been in my life for over 10 years. We had shared a lot of our life together and I was very familiar with him. The thought of being married to my husband was nice and it brought me relief. I thought that our marriage would last forever and that I would have someone to spend the rest of my life with. The reality was different, I married the wrong man and many of the things that I imagined, were purely images. An image can be made up in your mind, it can be viewed but it is not necessarily factual. The image that I had of being married did not equal my actual marriage. I remember, my husband and I had an argument, and he left the house for weeks. This was his routine and when things didn't go his way or became overwhelming for him, he left. This was not the first time that he left since we had gotten married. I can't recall what the argument was about, but I am pretty sure it had something to do with his mistress. He was gone for weeks, and I kept trying to tell myself that he was staying with friends or family. Maybe he needed space and eventually he would return to make things right. During this time, I literally walked around feeling as if I could barely breathe. Each breath I took felt as if it was a struggle and I was not getting adequate air into my lungs. I literally felt like half of me was gone and I would not be the same until it was returned. I had to be strong for my children at this time, faking a smile and making sure that they were okay. I also had to go to work despite not wanting to do anything but lay in bed. But that was not an option, because I knew that if my husband was not home, he definitely was not helping with any bills. I had to push through because life does not stop for anyone or any circumstance. I could have looked at this situation and realized that I was strong and that I did not need my husband. After all, he left and although it was hard, I kept going. I wasn't dead and I continued to take care of my responsibilities the best that I could. But instead, I allowed this situation to confirm my dependency on my husband. I thought about my breaths, my hurt feelings, and the constant pain that I was in for those weeks. I told myself that I needed my husband and that I would not feel better until he was home. Eventually, he came back home and instantly, I felt better. His presence made everything better, now I could go to work and smile and interact with my patients, instead of walking around like a zombie, faking it until I made it. At this point I was still weak; I was unaware of my strength and did not understand that I really did not need this man. It would take a few more arguments, a couple more disappearing acts and a book called *Letting Go* before I was finally able to realize that I did not need my husband. The first few times that he left it seemed like it made me weaker. But as he continued with the in and out, I begin to realize that I would be okay. I also read a book that would change my life and led me on a path to true happiness and unconditional love. This book helped me to see my situation in a different light. It is the first book that I ever read that emphasized that happiness should be from within. Happiness is not to be found in the things that we value in this world. This may sound crazy, making one question why they should not find happiness in their family, their children, their success, and so on. The answer to this question is that all of these things are temporary. If we place all our happiness in these external things, when they go away, there goes the happiness with them. That is not happiness and that is not how we should base our happiness. For instance, a woman may be happy that she received a promotion at her job. She is proud of herself, and the thought of her position makes her happy. The woman enjoys going to work and it truly brings her great joy. But what happens if the woman loses her job due to the downsizing of the company that she is working for? Now the woman is upset and worried about how she will take care of herself and her family. The woman now regrets taking the promotion and wishes she would have stayed in her old position. She feels as if all her hard work did not pay off and the woman has feelings of sadness and anger. The same job that once made this woman so happy now has her sad and upset. Just like that, the happiness is gone and honestly, it should not be. God did not put us on this earth to be sad, God is not sad so why would he want us to be? We are supposed to be happy, and we should be equipped to deal with all situations in life and continue to have happiness. I was not aware of this before reading this book, which explains this in detail. Happiness is a choice that can and should be chosen all the time. But we are so comfortable with choosing sadness or anger, or any feeling other than happiness. As soon as something does not go as planned or tragedy strikes, happiness is rarely chosen. I did not know how to choose happiness when my husband was not around. I choose to be sad and angry; I choose to be hurt and to keep telling myself that I needed him back home. All I could see was the need that I had for this man and nothing else really made sense. Thankfully, I read the book *Letting Go* and as I read the pages about happiness a voice came to me. The voice said to me that my husband and his mistress do not control my happiness. From that day on, I gained control of my life and instantly felt stronger. I would continue to repeat those words to myself, and I would continue to grow stronger. I realized that happiness was a choice and that I could always choose to be happy regardless of the circumstance. I also begin to consider that I did not need my husband like I thought I did. We all have a breaking point, some of us take longer than others but being fed up occurs eventually. My breaking point took years of bullshit from my husband. I truly put up with a lot of stuff with the belief that my husband loved me and that eventually we would be okay. As time went on, and with the realization that my husband was not my only source of happiness, I began to be comfortable with living without him. I continued to try to make my marriage work and I was not completely ready to let him go, but after reading the book, I just knew that I would be okay regardless of his presence in my life. Reading *Letting Go* led me to read other books that explained how our source of happiness can be found from within. I also began to read books about spirituality and our ego. The ego, that voice in our head that is constantly talking, usually attempting to be a victim and make the world all about itself. Attempting to shape the world from its point of view which can be extremely small and fictional. The ego wants to be in control and it wants to be needed by us.

We think we need this voice in our head, commentating on life's events. Honestly, it has been around since we can remember and seems to be a necessity for us to live. But the ego is not necessary to live and life without that voice would probably be better and more peaceful. The ego convinces us of our needs and tells us that we are alone and separated from one another. Everything that our ego convinces us that we need will only cause us pain. The needs of the ego will hurt us, if not immediately, they will eventually cause pain. I learned a lot about the ego and the issues that it can cause us in the book *A Course in Miracles*. An enlightening book that can help any individual that faces trials and tribulations in their life. My ego convinced me that I needed my husband. My ego would not allow me to let my husband go. I felt as if by letting my husband go, I would be losing. This is really not the case, if I would have disregarded the thought of needing him, I would have saved myself from a lot of pain. That voice in my head, that told me that I could not let another woman have my husband was insane. The ego is insane and thinks that it knows everything, but in reality, it knows nothing. I was insane to think that despite the cheating, lying and irresponsible behavior, my husband loved me. My marriage was not based on love, it was based on attachment. An attachment that is created by the ego, which does not know the true concept of love. Love does not need anything because it has everything. Love does not place expectations on anyone because it exists regardless of any circumstances. Love just is and always will be. Many of us do not know this type of love, we know attachments. We attach ourselves to one another and place expectations on each other. When these expectations are not met, love does not exist. I expected my husband to be a good man and to treat me right. I expected and needed my husband in order to be happy. When he did not meet these expectations, I did not feel loved by him. I choose all emotions but happiness due to his failure to meet my expectations. Love was non-existent in our marriage for many reasons. The main reason was that neither of us really knew how to love. I could not accept that my husband was not equipped or ready to be a husband. For me, love could only exist with us being married and us living the image that I built in my mind. The image was built by my ego, which does not know love, but is extremely familiar with attachment.

# CHAPTER 4

# I Was Broken

My second child was premature. I had to leave her in the hospital for a few weeks, and at the time it was the hardest thing that I had to do in my life. I was so heartbroken the day I left the hospital without her. I drove myself crazy until she came home. I could not sleep without her home and would call the nursery in the middle of the night just to check on her. I went back and forth to the hospital all day, every few hours to feed her, afraid that if she didn't see me or feel my touch that she would somehow not know that I was her mother. I didn't think I would ever experience a deeper pain than this. Years later I married a man that had no regard for my feelings. Making the pain that I felt the day I left the hospital without my newborn baby feel like nothing. During the time that I was married to my husband, I became broken. By the time the marriage was over, I was literally in pieces. My confidence was at zero, I felt as if I gave my all to this individual and it clearly was not enough. This made me feel as if myself as a whole was not enough to make another person happy. Of course, this was my ego's insane way of thinking and dealing with not getting what it wanted. I wanted my marriage to work, and it didn't. In the end when the final decision was made, the marriage was over, and my mind went into overload. My ego, with its insane thoughts, was on one thousand and I was at a low point in my life. I constantly heard those words repeated in my mind, "You are not good enough, you will never find love and will always be alone and your husband left you for the woman he loved, and that woman was not you!" In time, I would change my way of thinking and life would get better. This was a process and before going through that process to rebuild myself, I was broken. I was broken before my marriage officially came to an end. I begin to feel low during my first year of being married to my husband. As I married this man, there was really nothing that could prepare me for what was to come. The events that took place during my marriage had an everlasting impact on my life and how I viewed myself. Many times, I thought, I don't know if I will ever be the same after what I went through. I am pretty sure we all go through low points in our life and during this time, everything just seems painful. As humans, we develop hopes and dreams, with the idea that they will eventually come true. My dream was to live a happy life with my husband, who would love me and do right by me. I held on for as long as I could, keeping hope that things would change and get better. My husband and I would have good moments, but they would never last. Each time our happy moments were met with disappointment, I piece of me would chip away until literally, I was in complete pieces. Looking back on the days when I was in pieces, the only thing that could have kept me breathing was God. Without God, I would have been nothing because emotionally and mentally I was completely broken down. Being broken for me was having that constant nauseous feeling in my stomach. My heart would constantly race for long periods of time and my thoughts only produced negative feelings. When I did share happy moments with my husband, there was always this voice in the background reminding me of all the dirt he did. There was always an anticipation of my husband taking off and me not seeing him for however long. And the moments that he did leave, I would sit and pitifully wait for his return. I felt weak and I felt as if everything my husband was doing was my fault. To add to this, my husband was a big-time manipulator with an *I-can-do-whatever-I want-type-of-attitude*. Many of our fights that were about his infidelity would quickly be turned around on me. And each time my husband would manipulate me, I would fall for it and shift my energy. I would go from anger and fuck him to just trying to be a good wife and make my husband happy. I drained myself dry, trying to keep my husband happy. And at the end, I felt as if I had failed because after our last fight, he left, and the deci-sion was that the marriage was over. In the end, I lost myself and I had nothing to show for this loss. Looking at myself in the mirror, I did not recognize the image that was in front of me. My mother did not raise me to be weak and to take shorts from anyone. But I had taken two years of nothing but shorts, heartache, and pain. Going to school and receiving an education in mental health, I learned that our brains absorb everything and as we have experiences, we begin to operate in life based on our last experience. Our ego does not live in the present, it depends on our past to dictate our future. As we have experiences we begin to adjust to these experiences and move accordingly. If a child grows up in an abusive household, they become familiar with the abuse. It may seem normal to them, which leads them to be abusive in their own relationships as they grow. Their behavior is really not their fault, because they are doing what they know, the things that they learned. It is called learned behavior and basically, the brain takes in the experiences at home and projects them into the future. The result is that the child begins to expect the abuse, the child normalizes the abuse and the child expresses the abuse in other areas of its life. Everyone is different and the way in which they deal with any type of experience in their life can vary. One thing that is certain is that all experiences that we go through are processed through our brains and will impact our next move. The more and more my husband cheated, the more I expected him to cheat. I got to the point where I no longer believed that my marriage would work. I felt as if my husband would always cheat and that I would be stuck in a lifelong love triangle. The cheating kept taking place, so my brain began to normalize it and project it into the future. I no longer knew of a marriage that did not involve lies and infidelity. I still desired a marriage that was full of love and faithful-ness, but it was not my reality and along the way, hope was lost. My thinking process changed during my marriage, my ego went further and further into the future, taking past experiences with it to dictate the narra-tive. The broken self felt that I would never recover from the mess I experienced. Not only did my marriage fail, but life itself would be a complete failure. I felt this despite the success that I experienced; my marriage was a mess, but this was not the only area of my life. I was working on a Master's degree, holding down a 3.5 GPA. I locked down my dream job, working for the State, which came with wonderful benefits and good pay. I had two wonderful daughters who always made me smile. I did have success and good things going on in my life. But in the midst of this failed marriage, the good stuff just didn't overshadow the bad. This is why I say I was broken because all I could see and focus on was negative. All that I knew was that I was not good enough to make my husband do right and love me. This thought controlled me for a long time, and it would take some time to come back from such a low point. Our thoughts stick with us, and they have a lot of power, more than we know. As I went through my marriage, not only did the experiences break me. My own thoughts began to break me, and I don't know which was worse. The treatment that I received from someone that I expected to love me or the thoughts coming from my own brain. One thing that I learned, is that to begin emotionally and mentally broken can be exhausting and hard to heal from. I would rather have scars from physical abuse because once they are healed, they can pretty much be forgotten. The pain is gone, and you move on from it. A person does not forget emotional scars. They stick with you and pop up sporadically. Emotional scars can be triggered anytime, any place, under any circumstance. At the beginning when my marriage was first over, I could be at my work desk and my husband would enter my thoughts and I would have a strong urge to cry. For the longest time, I could not even say the name of my husband's mistress, without feeling anger and my heart racing. Over time things did get easier, and today I can laugh at the thought of his mistress. But I still have moments of anger or sadness when I think of how my marriage and how it ended. I still wonder what I did in life to deserve such treatment and such a traumatic experience, one that was supposed to be built on love. I have come a long way, but I still have my moments. It's as if the bad experiences are ingrained in my mind and my ego does not and cannot let them go no matter how much time has gone by. But this is expected of the ego, being that it only wants to acknowledge the past and the future. And with the ego, the future is dependent on the past. The ego likes pain and sometimes, I think all the ego knows is pain. Part of my process to put myself back together was to stop taking the ego so seriously and to talk to God more. The more I did this, the better I felt, and I got to the point where I didn't even have to talk. Instead, I began to listen. I also began to reflect on my entire life and who I really was. I looked back on my childhood and confronted the unresolved emotions that I was holding onto. My failed marriage was not my first heartbreak, and it may not even be the most traumatic experience of my life. I feel as if I was born into this world deficient and my story begins with loss. At the time that I was born, my father was already deceased, and my older sister had been taken from my mother traumatically. Straight out of the womb and I was already missing out on some critical components of my life. I was born to a mother who was trying to feel a void and dealing with extreme loss. Maybe I was expected to feel that void, but as a mother, I know that I was not able to do that. Because you cannot replace one child with the next. I remember my mother telling me that when I was born, I was this light-skinned fat baby with freckles all over my face and neck. She goes on to tell me that when the nurse brought me into the room, she tried to give me back, adamant that I was not her baby. Now that I know what my mom went through just one year before my birth, I get and understand her action to the fullest. I looked nothing like my older sister and even though my mom loved me, I was not my sister and could not replace what was taken. My sister had been kidnapped from my mother a year before I was born when she was three months old. An experience that had little effect on me as a child, but as an adult has caused much sadness and many tears. Growing up, I knew that I had a sister that was taken, but I didn't fully understand what that meant. Once I had my first child, the situation with my sister began to mean more to me. I had this beautiful little baby, and I could not imagine life without her. My thoughts would instantly go to my mother and how she must have felt after the incident. I don't know how she was able to go on, because I would not have been able to live life after something so tragic. For a long time, I felt sorry for my mother and what she experienced. I also felt bad that I was not able to take away that pain with my presence. One day, I was able to acknowledge what was taken from me with that experience. I was not welcomed into this world by my big sister, wearing one of those big sister t-shirts that parents put on the older sibling when the new baby is born. I never cried over my sister as a child, I just knew that what had happened was not good. Once I got older, the tears came, and they came often. I cried many times thinking of how I missed out on a sister relationship. I get angry when I think of some selfish woman walking off with my sister not thinking of the pain, she would cause my mother and me. I get frustrated when I try to imagine the type of woman my sister is today and where and what she is doing. It is a grieving process that will never end, the emotions from this experience will never run out for me. I understand my mom's void because I have one too. It cannot be filled by my little brother, girlfriends, or any other relationship, no matter how meaningful or important. The fact is that I missed out on a very important relationship with someone that is supposed to be in my life. I wasn't able to experience a sister's love, the only memory that I have of my sister is attached to a reservoir of endless pain. I didn't only miss out on a wonderful relationship with my sister, I grew up without my father. My father would not be there to welcome me into the world. He passed away before I was born, in an airplane accident traveling to Germany for the military. This is the story that I was told about my dad and I do not know much more about him. I used to have a picture of him, that I would stare at for hours. Imagining that he was there and the things that we would do as daughter and father. As I grew older, the imaginary stories that I created in my mind became frustrating because I knew that they were only thoughts. Nothing that I imagined was going to come true because my father was dead. There was no way I could recreate him in my thoughts and bring him back to life. As I got older, my mother rarely spoke about my father and eventually, I lost the picture of him. I can still see him in my mind clearly and the thought of him instantly brings me to tears. It is very hard to think of how life could be if I had a father. I do not know how I miss and crave a person that I have never met, but I do. There is no relationship thus far that has been able to take away the pain I feel when I think of my father or my sister. I am a mother and I love my children so much. I have a wonderful mother who is my best friend and a very close relationship with my little brother. But I still feel as if I missed out on some wonderful relationships. I still feel cheated because I don't have those memories with my father and my sister. In a way, missing out on these relationships is more traumatic than my marriage. I never got a say with my father and sister, it just was. By the time I arrived in this world, they were gone and there was nothing I could do to get that back. At least I was able to fight for my marriage and provided the opportunity to have a relationship with my husband. I had no chance with my father or my sister, I was truly robbed. I came into this world, suffering a loss that I would not quite understand until I was older. It almost seems that I should be equipped to deal with the pain and disappointment that my husband caused. Because pain and loss have been a part of my life since day one. Even with the tragedy that I have experienced in my early life, I still wasn't able to deal with the treatment from my husband. The events that took place before I was born did not equip me with the ability to overcome the abuse I faced in my marriage. The experience did not hurt less because I was familiar with loss. It did not keep me from breaking down when I caught my husband cheating several times throughout our marriage. It did not speed up the process when my marriage was finally over, and I was left to pick up all my pieces. I was able to look back on my life and acknowledge the impact that these experiences had on me and continue to have on me. I am okay with it, and I embrace my emotions when they come up. If I want to cry over my father or sister, then I do just that. I let the tears flow and then I let the feelings go. I allow the feelings to come up whenever they desire, and I let them go as needed. I realize that these experiences are a part of my story and I do not need to smother anything that has to do with them. I must accept that this is my reality and that there is nothing I can do about it. This is the same for my marriage and the things I went through with my husband. I cannot change the past, nor do I want to. I do not have to go into the future with my past experiences, no matter what my ego thinks. I can honestly live in the present, which is where God is and accept that I am okay at the moment. This is much easier said than done, I will most likely think of my father and my sister for the rest of my life. I will reflect on my marriage from time to time also. I will have my moments when I try to plan my future and I may reflect on my past when doing so. It's a natural thing for me because it's something that I have been doing all of my life. But today I can acknowledge that there is another way of thinking. Today I understand that the past is the past and it no longer exists. What does not exist, honestly does not need my energy. What does not exist cannot be taken into the next phase of my life. My past is not needed in my present, it has no place there and serves no purpose. My future can be left up to God and there is really no need for me to stress about anything that God is in charge of because he can be trusted to care for us and give us what is best for us. I did not understand this when I was broken, all I knew was that things were not going my way. The plans that I made were not working out and this was a problem for me. I tried so hard to live out my vision because I did not want to accept that God's vision was better. I did not want to let go of my marriage because I felt the need to understand God's plan before following it. This is what led me to experience pain and devastation. It led me to being broken and in pieces at the end of my marriage. I wanted what I wanted, and I couldn't see another way, I was rigid in my thinking. I read a book written by Neale Donald

Walsch, *Conversations with God*. In this book, God informs the author that he speaks to us through our experiences. (Walsch, 1997). The things that we experience in life have messages and many times we do not pay attention. I did not want to listen to God's messages, and it led to my suffering. I choose the hard way and in the end, my worse fear became my reality. I tried so hard to keep my husband home, I tried so hard to get my husband to love me. In the end we did not make it, God was communicating with me throughout my whole marriage, but I would not listen. I chose to hear what I want to hear, not realizing that in the end, God would win anyways. Honestly, love requires no effort, which I should have acknowledged in the beginning. I truly do not know why I wanted this man so badly, that I suffered for years, tearing myself down to keep him. Maybe it was that my husband was all that I knew, he brought a level of comfort to my life that I was too afraid to give up. I thought I knew what love was, but I did not truly understand love until after I was married. I surely was not loving myself, allowing this man to treat me in such a way that broke me down in every way. Love does not hurt, and it does not have expectations. I had expectations of my husband, and he did not meet them. He didn't even come close to meeting my expectations. My expectations and his shortcomings led to my misery, and it did not have to be this way. If only I had listened to God and trusted in his plan a little sooner.

After all is said and done, I could never really be broken. I perceived myself as broken and this led me to the feeling of brokenness. The feeling of being in pieces and not knowing how to get me back together. Thankfully, perception is not the truth, perception is subjective.

I may see things one way, while the next person in the same situation may see things in an entirely different way. Our perceptions are personal, and they are not consistent from person to person. This inconsistency makes perception not true. Instead it is just the way in which we view the situation or person. Perception can change at any time, one minute I felt broken but later I would feel whole again. Reality and truth do not change, it cannot change, it literally just is. The reality was that I am love, no matter what I perceived. Love does not fail, and love does not change, it is constant, and it always wins. When it comes to love, it is always there, it just depends on rather or not we want to accept reality or not. I was not broken because God did not make me broken. He made me to love and to be loved, just as he is. Once I was able to accept this reality, this truth, I was able to begin my recreation. I finally was able to get to the good stuff, I allowed myself to perceive life differently and to acknowledge my true self.

# CHAPTER 5

# I Had to Let it Go

Breakups can be hard, nobody wants to let go of that one person whom they thought they would spend the rest of their life. That person brings them so much comfort that imagining life without them instantly lowers their energy level. I always imagined myself getting married one time and living the rest of my life with that person. Divorce was never an option for me once I was married. And even after our final break up and I decided that I was done, the thought of divorce made me sick. This could not be happening, my marriage to my childhood love was over. My husband and I broke up in February 2020, we got into a huge fight early in the morning while he was on his way to work. It's funny because the whole fight started over a charger. Yes, our marriage finally came to an end over a cell phone charger. Neither my husband nor I are morning people, so it's always been a fragile time for us. I typically am quiet in the morning until I get myself together. I have never enjoyed getting up at 5:30 am to bring my husband to work, so you can only imagine how I was feeling after this man started yelling and cussing at me over a phone charger. This argument began in our house, continued in the car on the way to my husband's job and finally ended with a physical fight in our home. My husband could not find his charger which he is known for losing. The man loses everything and would probably lose his head if it wasn't attached to his body. He attempts to place his lost charger in my youngest daughter's possession and demands that I go get it out of her room. When I came back from her room empty-handed, his anger level ros and he began to yell at me. I don't remember exactly what he said. But I remember his aggression and I did not like his tone. He clearly had an attitude and was deciding to take it out on me. It only got worse from here; my husband decided he wanted to stop at his mother's house to get his charger. All of a sudden, he realized that this is where he had left his charger from the day before. So although I was tired and all I wanted to do was drop this man off and get back in my bed so I could get a few more hours of sleep before I would start my day, I drove to his mother's house. We argued the whole way to her house and continued to argue as I was pulling up to the house. Again, I cannot remember his exact words, but he said some slick and disrespectful words before exiting the car into his mother's house. So, I rolled down the window and yelled something back at him. Well, his mother must have heard me yelling at him because when he entered into the car he had a message from her. Whatever she said, rubbed me the wrong way and I was not letting it go today. Before I continued with my response and the remainder of this argument, I must mention that I love my mother-in-law. Throughout my marriage, my mother-in-law was very supportive and we had a wonderful relationship. But today was not the day and I was not in the mood for this bullshit. Her son had been cussing me out since I woke up and now her. I did something that I would not normally do, I pulled up in my mother-in-law's driveway and gave her a piece of my mind. How dare she comment on something that she knew nothing about. After all, her son started this mess first thing in the morning over a charger, that he misplaced. I yelled out for her to mind her business and told her if she would have raised her son right, we wouldn't have all these problems in our marriage. Of course, my response was coming from somewhere else, it was not about the fact that she commented on me yelling at her son. It was more than that, I was fed up. It was as if every text message I found, all the lies that were told and every disrespectful moment in my marriage rushed back to me at that moment. Up until now, I had dealt with a lot of bullshit, some things many of our family members may not be aware of. And now my husband's mother had a slick comment for me, without even addressing her son and his nonsense. I could not control myself and after I yelled at her, I felt relief. I wanted to slap the hell out of my husband and tell him to get out of my car and walk his ass to work. But that's not what happened, my husband was outraged by what I did. He instantly got on the phone with his oldest sister and told her that I yelled at their mother. He then proceeded to talk about me with his sister as if I was not sitting right there. Another fight in which everything gets turned around on me. Nobody acknowledged my feelings, there was no discussion about me being yelled at and my daughter being accused of something that she did not do. None of that mattered, the focus was that I had yelled at his mother and that I was wrong. I became more and more infuriated with my husband. He continued to yell at me and told me he was going to have his sister whip my ass when I dropped him off. I was in disbelief; how dare he threaten me with his sister. But that was not all, he continued to rant as I drive, yelling that he would do whatever he wanted and that there would be nothing I could do about it. At this point I had enough, I could not take another minute with this man. I drove us home and the arguing continued. It turned physical, I don't know who hit how first, but my husband and I begin to fight. We got at it for a few minutes, hitting each other and talking shit to one another. I was pissed at this point; our room was turned upside down and everything was a mess. All this over a charger, I cannot believe this. Finally, we stopped and I was on the floor near our bed and my husband was on the floor near the door. There was silence and my husband told me that I better say something to him, or it was over. I didn't have the strength to speak one word and I wanted as much distance as possible from this man. I was tired and I had no more fight in me. I stayed quiet and my husband walked away. He went into the next room and made a call. Finally, he began to pack his things and now I was panicking. For a moment I tried to talk to him and get him to stop packing, this is when he said the most meaningful words he had ever said to me. I can still hear these words as if he is standing right in front of me and yelling them. He told me he was leaving, and I just needed to let him go. At that very moment, I decided that I was done, I was not chasing this man and I was going to do what he asked. Those words spoke volumes, up until now, I always had hope that my husband loved me and deep down he wanted to be with me. But he asked me to let him go and I had to respect that. I needed to hear those words because they confirmed my worst fear; my husband did not want to be with me. For the next few weeks, I heard those words, in my mind and they were my driving force to keep looking forward and let this marriage go. His words were my motivation and this was the last time my husband would leave me. I promised myself that this would be the last time and the only way that I could ensure this was to never take him back. I was done. I had my weak moments when I really wanted to call him and fix things. But I would replay those final words and instantly change my mind. Another thing that really stuck out and hurt me that morning was my husband talking about me to his sister. He had every intention for his sister to fight me and that hurt. I was his wife; he was supposed to be my protector but instead, he went to great lengths to hurt me. His mistress had shown up to our daughter's job, she had even shown up to my job once. She disrespected me numerous times and he never reacted. He never let me touch her, he went to great lengths to protect her. But here he was, more than willing to call his sister on me, his wife. I replayed that morning and my husband's actions and words over and over for months. Finally, I understood and the picture was super clear. My husband did not love me and he clearly has a soft spot for his mistress. I felt this for a long time but I kept telling myself no, that this could not be. I could no longer tell myself that there was love within my marriage after that morning. The events that took place that morning really allowed me to see that my husband did not care about me. I was hurt every time I thought of how he protected his mistress but was so quick to jump on me. And after we fought, I had this horrible mark on my face, visible for everyone to see. Every time I looked in the mirror, I felt like Tina Turner, in that scene after she fought Ike in the limo. She looked at her face in that hotel room and finally had enough. Well, my mark was nothing like Tina's, but I had that moment when I saw my face and that mark on my cheek. I was done, it was time for me to let this mess go. I had no more fight in me and really there was nothing left to fight for. This marriage was over before it even started. I was a fool the whole time, chasing a man that did not want me and did not love me. Now it was time for me to start loving myself and get myself back together again. The first few months were hard after I made the decision to let my marriage go. I had no idea what I was going to do next. But I knew that I was not going back to my husband. I no longer was concerned about his whereabouts and did not care if he was with his mistress. I was so done that I had a date for Valentine's Day. A few weeks prior to our breakup, I was in the store and a guy gave me his number. I didn't think much of it at the time, I really respected my marriage despite the fact that my husband sucked. I took my wife's role seriously and would never cheat on my husband. I did take the guy's number with no plans of using it. A few weeks later, the fight occurred and I no longer had a reason not to use this number. So, I did, I made the call and here I was back in the dating game. I didn't have to spend my first Valentine's Day since the breakup alone and actually had lots of fun with my new friend. I also decided to see a therapist to help me get through this process. I told my family that I was done with my husband, and I began my process of moving on. At the same time as my breakup, I was also losing my house and it was time to move out. I was dealing with a lot and a part of me expected my husband to reach out and offer to help with the move. Of course, that never happened but I made it just fine without him. To add to all my stress, someone decided to call DCF on me and reported that my husband had drugs around my kids. I wonder who that could have been, being that I just got into it with my husband's family. Here I was, marriage was over, moving out of my house which I worked so hard to get, and a DCF case based on a false claim. I felt like crap, but I knew that I had to push through. I cried every morning on my way to work. From the time that I got in the car until I got off at the exit, I cried for days. As I pulled into the parking lot of my job, I would wipe my tears, enter the building with a smile on my face and get my work done. No one knew what I was going through, and I kept it that way. By March, Covid hit the United States and many states were beginning to shut down. My job sent us home to work and I was thankful to be alone. I was also thankful to still have my job, being that many people were out of work due to this virus. My job was considered essential, and it was set up so that we could work from home. I also found a nice condo to rent and was able to move out of my mother's apartment about one month after moving in. My DCF case was closed, with no abuse or neglect found. Things were getting better for me, I continued to talk to my male friend, had weekly appointments with my therapist and was reading every spiritual book that I could get my hands on. I did not call my husband and tried my hardest to keep him and his mistress out of my thoughts. I had my good days and my bad days but I was moving on. I prayed to God, begin to meditate and surrounded myself with people that cared for and loved me. I knew that I had to let the bad things in my life go. I could no longer pretend that my marriage was going to be okay. I knew that no matter what I did, it just was not meant for me and my husband to be together. I had sat with love and experienced it, fought with it and been let down by it. I had gotten in bed with love, I was intimate with it. I had even conquered it for a while, I felt it, was hurt by it, cried over it, and finally, I defeated it. Love as I had known it, and now I was done. I didn't want the love that I knew. I wanted something different, the love that comes with peace. The love that requires nothing and only brings joy, that is what I desired. The war was over, and I had to accept that I lost this one. Excuse my French, but I got fucked up fighting this war, I may have won a few battles but overall, I had lost. I gladly waved my white flag and surrendered. I also knew that this was my very last battle and the last war I would ever take part in. I lost and now I was done. I decided to get up, with all my scrapes, bumps, and bruises and move on. I also decided to never fight again because I acknowledged that I do not have to fight. There is another way, and that is love. With that being said, I decided to love myself more than hate my husband. In letting go of my marriage and the past, I was able to focus on myself and the positive things in my life. I woke up with my ego each morning and choose to push through. I did not allow the irrational thoughts to get to me. I knew that listening to my ego would only cause more pain and get me nowhere. Instead, I would meditate and learn to differentiate between the ego and my spirit. I was no longer interested in what my ego had to say. I wanted the voice of love because it would bring me peace. In letting my marriage go, I felt lighter. It was a hard decision to make, there was nothing that I wanted more than to be with my husband. I cannot stress that enough, I really tried to keep my marriage together, but I was the only one trying. My husband and I were not on the same page and for whatever reason, it just was not working out. My husband reached out to me one time after our last argument. It was a weird encounter and I really knew that I was done. Usually, when my husband would reach out after an argument, I would get excited and instantly think of how we could get things right again. But this time there was a lack of interest, I was still in my feelings about the things that took place that morning of our last fight. I did not want to be bothered but somehow this man found his way back to the house. I hadn't moved out yet, so he still knew my location. He came over and spent the night, which was uneventful. We didn't talk much and I really don't know why he was there. The next morning, early, he had me drop him off at his cousin's house. We sat in the car for a few minutes and my husband stared at me, he asked me if I missed him and if I wanted to hear from him later. I gave him an emotionless "Yeah" he must have felt it. We made eye contact one last time and as I looked at him, I knew that this would be the last time that I would see my husband. I felt strong energy, and I knew that it was over between us. I looked into his eyes, and I did not feel anything. I didn't feel love or happiness, I didn't feel pain or sorrow. It was just nothing, I was empty of all emotions. My husband exited the car and I never heard from him again. Seven months later, in September 2020, I would receive divorce papers from my husband. When I received them, I felt nothing, I was not sad and there was no pain. I signed the papers and sent them back in, relieved that everything would officially be over soon. It would take almost a year to get a court date to finalize our divorce. During that time, I continued to move on from the past. Things got easier and easier for me. The sadness and anger died down and became further and further in-between. Eventually, I began to go weeks without thinking about my husband. I began to hold my husband in my prayers and to think of him during my meditation, sending him positive energy. I even began to pray for his mistress from time to time and no longer had a strong urge to hurt her. In time, I felt lighter, I was happy and I reflected on the months since my breakup and realized that life had gotten much better. Letting go of my marriage turned out to be a good thing for me, it was a benefit and gain rather than a loss. I was so afraid of being without my husband, but from the moment that we split, I was just fine. I didn't fold, I didn't die, I survived, and I was okay. I didn't go to bed thinking about where my husband was and what he was doing. I didn't have that nauseous feeling in my gut and no more racing heartbeats for no reason. My family noticed a difference in me and my kids were happier also. They didn't have to watch their mother be stressed out and hurt anymore. My moods were better and overall I just felt better. I was so afraid of getting a divorce but when I received my divorce papers, I did not feel fear. I remember one day when I first moved into my new place, I was sitting in the living room, crying. I had been emotional that day, I missed my husband and was upset that my marriage was over. I would have days like this from time to time for the first year after we split. As I cried this day, I asked God to help me, I told God, if he didn't want me to be with my husband, that I would need some help. I asked God for strength and love to get through this. I asked him to take this feeling away and help me to get through this without so much pain. I didn't want to feel this pain anymore, I was tired of crying and feeling sad. I was sincere and very clear that day about what I wanted from God as I cried out to him. Things got easier from that day on. I still had my moments but nothing like that day. God answered my prayer, he heard me that day and made sure that I was okay. He didn't bring my husband back into my life, he provided me with the strength and understanding to move on. This was another moment that confirmed that my husband and I were not meant to be together, and I accepted it. Acceptance is very important, especially when life brings you hardship. Fighting against a situation that is already occurring is like swimming against a strong current in the middle of the ocean. All you do is use up all your energy just to end up exactly where the current wants to take you. And I can't even swim, so being in the middle of the ocean fighting against anything just makes no sense. It was the same for my marriage at this point. There was no need to ignore all the signs and to try to convince me of anything other than the relationship is over. I was finally able to accept this and trust in God that I would be okay despite the hardships that I faced. Honestly, accepting that my marriage was over made the situation easier to handle. I was going with the flow and allowing myself to just live. This is how I know that life can be easier when we don't fight. When we let go and accept our circumstances, perception changes, daily tasks become easier and feelings are more bearable. I didn't have to go through life on the defense. Instead I was able to focus on love and getting to a peaceful place in my life. When I was married, I was focused on my husband and all the bad things that I felt he was doing to me. Once it was over and I was able to accept that it was over, there was no more taking him back and trying to make it work. There was no more getting upset when things did not work out and he back to cheating again. With acceptance I was able to break a horrible cycle that was literally tearing me to pieces. If I did not accept what God was telling me, I would still be in the disgusting marriage trying to make things work. Only God knows where I would be if I did not decide to let this marriage ago and accept that this was not what was meant for me. My only regret-if I had to have one-would be that I did not accept what God was communicating with me a lot sooner.

# CHAPTER 6

# Recreation Of Me

In letting go of my marriage, I was able to focus on myself. Reflecting back on my marriage, I realized that being with my husband was a disservice to myself. Being with him and loving him, left me in a mess- a complete and empty mess. I was no longer going to love another at my own expense. I should not have to and that is not what love is all about. Anyone who, including myself at a point in time, feels that love is about sacrifice and that it involves pain or suffering. They must think again and reassess the components of love. Love is effort- less, it requires nothing and exists everywhere. Love does not involve pain, and there is no suffering where love exists. There just isn't, love does not have to defend itself and there is no fear where loves lie. Love feels good and it is not questionable. There is nothing to think about when it comes to love, it exists and wherever love is, feel- ings of happiness and peace exist also. My marriage was not built on love and honestly, I don't know what the hell its foundation was. I did know that I had to love myself back to being a functioning person. I realized that I was important and deserving of someone who was willing to give me what I am capable of giving them-love. Once my marriage was over, I was able to understand this, and I made a promise to myself to keep myself first. From the day that I had my last fight with my husband, I began to love myself more than I ever had. In a way, I felt as if I needed to replenish myself from being drained during the last few years. In the beginning, it was hard to do anything and I just wanted to know why my marriage did not work out. I have always been the type of person that needed an explanation for anything that occurs. It has always been a *why this* and a *why that* with me, and my marriage ending was no different. Eventually, I would get my answer and it was simple. My husband was not going to bring me peace. I remember one day, I was sitting in silence, practicing quieting that voice in my head that is constantly going. I sat there for some time, possibly 5 minutes which felt like 30 minutes. This is when I was in the beginning stages of meditation and silence in my head for 5 minutes was a true accomplishment. I remember my first thought after the 5 minutes of quietness. The thought was a question to God, why didn't my marriage work? Following this thought, as clear as day, the words *HE WAS NOT GOING TO BRING YOU PEACE* came into my head. This was God letting me know that being married to my husband was not really what I wanted. Peace is something that I have always wanted, it's always been a goal to have a life that was peaceful. I did not have peace during my marriage, and I was not going to get it while being in a relationship with this man. At the end of the day, my husband was not worth my peace, no one is worth another person's peace. Peace lies with love and a marriage that is full of love will have peace. This was hard to grasp at first because my vision was to have my husband and to have peace. But that just was not how things were going to work. And once I was able to accept this, things got easier. From that day when God spoke those words to me, it became easier for me to accept my failed marriage. I developed a better understanding of why things did not work out and I was able to begin my process of moving on. If I ever must decide between my peace and a person, I am choosing my peace hands down. Because at the end of the day any person in my life that truly loves me, won't disturb my peace anyways. So, after acceptance came the recreation of myself. I was able to accept that this marriage was over, and I was able to come to terms with it. But now I had to move on and get myself together and be even better than I was before, because why not? It was time for the recreation of myself. When you recreate something, the end result is in your hands. You have full control of the direction this thing that you are creating is going in. If you are redecorating your bedroom, you get to decide the new space for the bed and what color scheme to use. The decisions are yours and they can truly be endless. By the time my husband and I split, I realized that I was the worse version of myself. At this point, I had no choice but to rebuild myself and become whole again. My recreation was necessary because there was no way that I was going to remain the same person I was as I went through the mess. By doing that I would be holding on to something that was no longer, and the misery would continue. There was no way after the events that I went through that I would be the same person that I was before. It just was not possible and this too, I had to accept. In the midst of my marriage, I perceived myself as broken into pieces. It was a perception but at the time, it felt extremely real. I had no idea that my true self could never be harmed. So, with the perception of being broken came the idea of being put back together again. The pieces that I had broken into during the past few years, I kept every last one of them. Each time a piece of me broke off during an argument, reading a text message, or waiting for my husband to come back home, I picked that broken piece up and saved it. It's as if I knew that I would need that piece again one day for my recreation. One day I would be able to put all these pieces back together and recreate myself into a masterpiece. And that is exactly what I did, I recreated myself beginning by taking a look from within. I took time to reflect on myself and who I really was. This is something I never did before, I never took the time to really figure myself out. Up until this point, I was a surface person. I never went deep to get to know what was truly best for me and what I really wanted in life. I just followed that voice in my head and went with it. I realized that this got me nowhere but heartache and suffering. Coming out of such a devasting event, I knew that I had to make changes that would ensure that I would never have to experience such trauma ever again. Letting go of my marriage I took back control of my life, my feelings, and myself. This was a good feeling. Despite the sadness I felt when the marriage came to its official end, it felt good to have control again and to know I had endless options in recreating myself. The new me, the me that was re-pieced back together, I had to make sure the end product would be the best version of me. All those little pieces had to go back together perfectly and I was going to take my time and make sure of it. At this point, I was in my new place, my girls were happy, and I was getting back to a good mental state to begin my process. I also had a nice flow of emotional support from friends, family, and my therapist, along with the start of my spiritual journey. There was no better time to start this recreation and I would have been a fool to just stay stuck and remain the same person that I had become during my marriage. I begin reading books that discussed spirituality and when the time was right, I began the daily assignments found in A *Course of Miracles*. To this day, I feel that this is one of the best and most productive things that I could have done in my life. In the beginning, I didn't really understand these assignments but that is the good thing about A *Course of Miracles*. You truly do not need to understand anything, there only needs to be an open mind and wiliness to accept a new way of thinking. God will do the rest and meet you where you are, there is no failure involved and you can only gain. It's funny because sometimes when we are at our lowest, that is when blessings come rolling in. God does not take anything away; we just perceive loss and incorporate it with God taking something from us. This is really not the case, but there are times when certain things have to happen to prepare us for better things or for the things that we really want in life. It can feel like a loss, but once all is said and done, the final result is so rewarding that the things that we feel we lost suddenly have no value. If the value can be so easily susceptible, how valuable was it in the first place? When we perceive loss yet allow God to be in control and go with the flow, the reward can only be great. As I started my recreation process, I began to feel better and it did not take long for this to happen. My new self was able to acknowledge my emotions, positive or negative and let them flow. I learned how to let my emotions happen yet stand behind them and eventually let them go. I was no longer having these negative emotions and identifying with them. I would acknowledge my sadness or anger and then envision that emotion as it moved along. There was no longer the desire to just be sad and feel sorry for me because things did not go my way. The new me was learning to go with the flow of life. Accepting my feelings and learning to no longer identify with them was refreshing, it was smart. By identify I mean if I was sad one day, I was not going to just sit there and be sad all day. Instead, I would acknowledge that my current mood is sad, accept that I was sad and move on from it. I was no longer just sitting in sadness for hours or days at a time. Each time the feeling of sadness came up, I would just let it sit there for a moment and literally say okay, now you can go. Eventually, the particular feeling stopped coming up as often until one day, even the painful thoughts of the past no longer created sadness in me. It took some time to get to this point, but I stayed persistent and relied on God along with my support group to get me to the next stage of this process. There was no need to just sit in sadness over something that I have no control over or something that no longer mattered. I was learning to let life be what it was going to be. In the recreation of myself, I learned so much about who I truly was. As I took a deeper look into myself, for the first time I was able to recognize my triggers. I also developed a better understanding of my behavior and the way I moved. I began to pay attention to my tone of voice and the words I used when communicating. I also began to explain myself to my loved ones, when I caught myself being overly aggressive or emotional. I began to appreciate the people who stuck it out with me and acknowledged their love for me. Which made me want to be good to them and explain myself whenever I was not doing anything other than showing them love. The best feeling came when my family actually saw a change in me which only motivated me more to continue to develop into the best version of myself. I didn't only acknowledge and work on myself in the areas that needed some attention. I also developed a better understanding of my happiness and what love meant to me. During my recreation, I made sure to surround myself with the people that showed me love and support. It felt good and today, I am not willing to be around anything less. I refuse to engage in unhealthy relationships and no longer lower my standards for anyone to be in my life. When I recreated myself, I learned to be okay with being alone. Being alone has always been my worse fear, and to this day, I do not want to grow old alone. At the same time, during my process of healing, I learned to be okay and enjoy alone time. I would rather be alone than surround myself with people who are not genuine or act on anything less than love. My recreation was a success and many times I wonder who I would be today if I did not go through this process. I began my process with tears and pain that seemed endless. Therefore, it only seemed right to recreate me with strength that was also endless. Today I am strong and I am aware. I know who I am and I know what I want. I am no longer willing to settle for anything less. I understand that I do not have to and that my life can be and will be the way that I envision it- full of peace and love.

# CHAPTER 7

# The Come Up

My final breakup with my husband was in February 2020. Being so close to the holiday, I just knew that I was going to have a miserable Valentine's Day. The crazy thing is that I never celebrated Valentine's Day when I was married or anytime during my relationship. My husband was one of those people that lived by the model that every day is Valentine's Day. But the thought of spending this Valentine's Day without him stressed me out. Not only was I going to have an upsetting Valentine's Day, but I was also anticipating the next few months to be rough. My husband was my norm and we all know that the beginning stages of a breakup are the worse. Even if the relationship was unhealthy, it was mine and I would have to mourn the perceived loss. Because at the time of the breakup, I definitely felt like it was a loss for me. I would have to adjust to our end, because this time, I was not letting him come back and deep down I knew that our marriage was officially over. With this knowledge came fear and anxiety about what is next for me. I knew that I was not going to jump into another relationship immediately, but I also knew that I needed something to help me get over my current state. I was overwhelmed when we first broke up but I was also angry. The events that took place during my last fight with my husband were my motivation. There was no way in hell, I was going back to a man that was willing to call his sister to fight me and that would sit in my face and just talk negatively about me like I was nothing. I reflected on the last fight we had a lot and every time it made me so upset, that I truly could not fathom the idea of ever being with him again. I also reflected on all the things that I went through during my marriage and each time I came to the same conclusion- the bad outweighed the good. I would not be going back to that hot mess of a relationship. And although I felt sadness and confusion, I also felt a sense of relief. Getting back to Valentine's Day, I did not spend it being miserable at all. I actually had a wonderful Valentine's Day and spent it with someone who would end up being an important part of my process. An individual that today I consider to be a friend and that I would not hesitate to call for anything. I went out on a nice date for Valentine's Day with a wonderful person with who I developed a great relationship. It's funny how the universe aligns things up so nicely at times. Actually, the universe always works in our favor but many times we as humans are so confused, we don't realize our favor even if it was sitting next to us in the car. Everything happens for a reason, and I was in the store at the same time with this man for a reason. He had the confidence and will to approach me and give me his number for a reason. And the sun and the stars aligned nicely, leading me to have the confidence and will to use his number. It was the start of something wonderful and I am extremely happy that I crossed paths with this new man. Talking and texting led to a date, which happened to be on Valentine's Day. It was very nice, to be out with a man that was responsible and handsome and basically nothing that I experienced in a very long time. This new guy was nothing like my ex, and it felt great. I felt good that I was able to attract a decent man, I also felt great that I had someone that showed interest in me without all the extra drama. For the past two years, I shared my man with another woman, and it really messed me up. This new man was not my boyfriend, he was not my husband. But interactions with him were new and they felt good- there was no worrying with my new friend. In addition to having something new, this man was really a good catch. Not only was he handsome, he was also smart-currently working on his bachelor's degree. He had multiple cars, his own place and only one child. He worked an honest job and was in a position to take care of himself. We had wonderful conversations leading up to our date, along with enjoying each other's company on Valentine's Day. Interacting with this new man kept me distracted and it definitely played a part in me not going back to my ex. For some reason, it was a surprise to me that there were good black men still in the world. Don't get me wrong, I love my black men and acknowledge that there are many wonderful black men in the world. But being in the presence of one after my marriage was a shock for me. A shock that was very much welcomed and necessary for my process. I was not going back to my ex before I met this new guy, but after I met him, it sealed the deal. I was one thousand percent not going back to my ex and I was completely okay. I would continue to have my moments of sadness, anger or just wondering why I married such a man. But this new man gave me hope and made my process a little bit easier. We never left the friend zone, but we were able to develop a wonderful friendship full of good times and laughter. Although he is a very good man, he faced his own trauma in a relationship. Due to his past, he had absolutely no desire to be in a relationship. It really didn't matter, because we still established something special and having him around helped my process in many ways. Being around this man motivated me to get out and start dating. I realized that I did not have to sit around mourning a loss or my marriage that was over. I had options and it was time to weigh them. I realized that my life was not over, just getting started. This super cold, named COVID-19 came into town and shut things down, literally. So yes, I was ready to get out there and start dating, the world literally shut down and here I was sitting in the house. Around the same time as the shutdown began, I also began to realize that this new guy and I would not be taking it any further than friends. As I said, I was okay with this, but I also acknowledged that I needed a little more. It was like I had a little taste of something good, but I wanted the whole plate. My options were limited being that my life along with everyone else's life was limited to Walmart, the gas station, and our homes. This was okay though because the universe had my back and it all worked out. One day, I was scrolling through social media and noticed an old friend. The voice in my head suggested that I reach out but I was reluctant. I'm not the slinging-in-any-man's DM's type of girl. It took me a few days but finally, I did reach out by sending my old friend a message. During the days of contemplation, I kept thinking of him and reflecting on all our past memories. We were just friends in the past, yet every interaction was nice and refreshing. Finally, I decided to reach out because I just wanted to be around someone familiar and nice. At the very least we could have a conversation full of reminiscing and laughter. There was also the idea that my old friend has other male friends and who really knows how that could end up. Once I got the nerve to reach out, I got an instant reply and that was all he wrote. Another wonderful relationship, this one I will say was re-established. My old friend and I had about fifteen years behind us at this point. We began talking and literally picked up where we left off. To this day, we speak every day by text message or phone. We also continue to see one another whenever possible being that we live in different states, a few hours away. Reaching out to my old friend was one of the best things that I did in the months after my breakup. This man was the truth and any lasting thoughts that I had about my ex, would soon disappear completely. Within a few months of reaching out to my old friend, I was like, "Ex-husband who ?" This man helped me to make more progress during my post-break-up and I have not looked back since. Since I was in my early twenties, I always loved Brooklyn, New York and strongly felt that there was something about a man from Brooklyn. Honestly, when I was marrying my husband who was not from Brooklyn, I was a little disappointed but at the time I felt my feeling was nonsense. After all, a region should not determine the love that one has for another. As I say that, I still strongly believe there is something about a man from Brooklyn. I have encountered many men from Brooklyn and each one has this swag or way about them that I have never experienced with a man from any other part of the world that I know. In addition to his natural ways, my old friend and I just mesh together really well. It's always a good time when we are together, and I truly enjoy every moment that we spend together. Being with him after my breakup was so refreshing and it was needed more than meeting my new friend in the store that day. In so many ways, my old friend helped to bring me back to life and as we developed something special, I began to give my ex less and less energy. Not only did I have two wonderful men in my life, one who was a wonderful friend and another whom I was building something special with. I also had many other things to look forward to. At some point, I realized that my ex was not my whole life and that I could live life without him. Not only could I live life without him, but I could also live a great life without him. My life was quite peaceful since my ex left and had less anxiety and anger. I developed positive relationships with men, and I was not worried about where I stood in anyone's life. It was a good feeling and there was no way that I would ever go back to a life that gave me anything less. It was just the men in my life that had me smiling and feeling better. I was more social, and despite the world being on lockdown, I was spending lots of time with new friends that I made at work. I also continued to work on my master's degree which took up lots of my time. I was reading every self-transformation or spiritual book that came within my reach. I also had my family around me which gave me so much assurance. My friends and family allowed me to remember that there was love in the world and especially there was love surrounding me. I didn't look back after my ex left the last time. Despite my fear of the unknown, I kept moving forward and remained determined to be happy and have peace. It did not take long for things to pick up for me once I made this decision. Every day was not a good day, I continue to have moments for some time after the breakup. But they were only moments, I did not allow them to be days or even hours. I was no longer going to allow another individual to cause me sadness or any negative feelings. As time went on, the moments became further and further between. At some point, the moments stopped altogether, I had made it. During my process, I was provided with the things I needed to keep going and remain strong. I didn't imagine my post-break-up to turn out the way it did. I am so grateful that the process was easier than I expected, and I never looked back. Through the process I came up, I realized my worth and I understood that love surrounds me. I no longer had to chase after anything. Instead I remained still and allowed everything to happen naturally for me. I allowed love to happen, because that is what it does, it just happens. There is no resistance, no flaws, no issues, or drama, love just is.

# CHAPTER 8

# Switching Things Up

Just like the beginning of something has its own characteristics. That good feeling is experienced when a relationship first begins, and it seems as if nothing can go wrong. The ending of something also comes with a set of characteristics. The ending indicates that the event is over and depending on what the event is and how it ends certain feelings may arise. The ending may not feel as good as the beginning, yet it can feel wonderful. The end of a relationship may produce an array of feelings, yet the end of a struggle may bring relief. The end of my relationship with my husband was tough. I experienced many feelings, I was sad that the relationship was over. I was also angry because I felt as if I had played myself, wasted time, and I felt as if my husband's mistress had won the war. I was worried that I would not bounce back and be able to experience love again. These are the feelings that I can put into words, I experienced other feelings also that were indescribable. In the end, I was really all over the place and had to force myself to take things day by day to keep myself somewhat together. I knew I was not taking part in the relationship anymore, so there were some feelings of relief that I would no longer have to fight or be subject to the mistreatment that my husband gave out effortlessly. The end was hard, to say the least, it felt nothing like the beginning when we had first begun to date. There was no feeling like nothing could go wrong because it had already gone horribly. The end represented the fact that I had tried and done all I could, but we did not make it. The end sucked and it was hard for me to control my feelings at first. It was hard for me to think straight and not have the urge to want to cause harm to my husband and his mistress. Thankfully I was able to switch it up, I was able to get myself together. I knew I had to switch it up because I could not continue through life in my current feelings. In the months of the breakup, I was tense, and I wanted my husband to be miserable. I would think of him or his mistress and just wish harm on them. At this point, my thoughts were that they were both horrible people and deserved to be punished. I would have visions of God punishing my husband for treating me so badly during our marriage. I would replay God reminding him of all the bad things he did and banishing him to hell in my mind a few times a week. I strongly felt that this man would have no good luck and that God was disappointed in him for his role as a husband. After all, how could God love such a horrible person that made vows and did not respect them? It's funny how the brain works and creates these thoughts that we identify with and truly believe. As a therapist, I am aware that our brain basically functions on what it experienced in the past. That voice in our mind makes statements based on what happened previously. Basically, the past is all that it knows, so this is what it uses to provide its "advice". For example, the very first time that my husband pulled some funny stuff, I had no idea what was happening. My mind could not conceive that my husband would be cheating on me because at this point I still did not have a name, a face, or any legit information to prove his cheating. It was a rainy night, and I was laying in bed getting ready to fall asleep. My husband was in the family room, watching TV and plotting unbeknownst to me. He comes into the bedroom as he is talking on the phone telling someone he will not be coming out because it's too late. Later I would find out, that he wasn't on the phone with anyone, this was his decoy. He was honestly playing games and trying to make me think one of his guy friends was trying to get him to come out for some drinks. He hangs up the phone and begins to talk to me for a few minutes. He then proceeds upstairs to the kitchen; this would be the last time I would see my husband for the rest of the night. He was supposedly going upstairs to get something to drink but he never came back. I think I dozed off for a few minutes waiting for him to come to bed. A loud thunder woke me up from my sleep and I realized that he had not returned. Thinking to myself that it does not take that long to get a drink from the kitchen, I get up to see what is happening. I go into the kitchen and the back door is wide open. It almost looked like a home evasion has taken place, but the only thing that was missing was my husband. I was in shock and completely clueless as to what just happened. I even stepped outside quickly and there was no sign of my husband. I called his phone and got nothing. I believe it went straight to voicemail. Not one time did I think that my husband had just left the house to go be with his mistress. My thoughts were more on his well-being. Was my husband okay, I honestly imagined him somewhere in the woods hurt and needing me. Needless to say, I did not sleep well that night. In the morning I got up and forced myself to go to work, despite the fact that my husband still had not returned home and was not answering his phone. I was thinking the worse, which currently was that my husband was dead somewhere in the woods. I called my father-in-law during my morning break to tell him about the weird incident that happened the night before and express my concern. Of course, he hadn't heard from him either and didn't have much feedback for me. Eventually, my husband would return home with no explanation as to what happened. A month or so later, I discovered the text messages in my husband's phone. I was able to put two and two together and realized what took place that night. My husband literally left the house and was picked up down the street by his mistress. He wasn't hurt in the woods; he was spending quality time with his mistress, not thinking about me at all. At that time, I would have never thought this was the case, that voice in my head was convinced that my husband was somewhere hurt. I am not sure if this was my way to cope with the incident at the moment and deep down, I really knew that there was some funny business taking place. I do know that after that moment, my views and thoughts begin to shift. I became more suspicious; my brain locked that experience in and moving forward would proceed with caution. Thinking about these moments, and there were many more that were way worse than disappearing into the night, led me to believe that my husband deserved to be punished. By the time our relationship came to an end, I had gone through so much that forgiveness seemed impossible and unnecessary. I had no reason to forgive this man for all the things that he put me through. First of all, he didn't apologize for any of the pain and destruction that he caused. To me, that meant he wasn't sorry, and he did not care. If this was the case, there was no need to forgive him. I was too much into my own feelings to want to forgive anyone even if they were sorry. Leading up to the final break up, I heard "I am sorry," and "This is the last time," so many times, that my husband could have shown up with an apology, but he was leaving with nothing this time. At the moment, forgiveness was just not possible for me. One thing that was clear after the final break-up was that it was final and there was no make up this time. This reality brought me relief and pain, along with the thought of me being a victim. Feeling like a victim, I felt that someone must pay, and that someone was my husband. Not only my husband but his mistress also. I imagined that they were together, where else would he go and stay away for so long? After the last time that I saw my husband, he never reached out again. It hurt to think of him with this other woman, knowing that he loved her more than he loved me. I wanted them both to experience the pain that I felt. I did not want them to be happy together, because I was not happy. On top of that, they didn't deserve happiness because they were bad people. These were my thoughts for the first few months after the breakup. Thankfully, I gave everything to God, my thoughts, my feelings, my hurt, my pain-EVERYTHING. He took it and turned it around for me and I am grateful. Despite the anger and hurt that I felt, I continued my spiritual journey and relied on God to provide me with insight and take care of me. I read a lot of books and took part in daily lessons from A *Course of Miracles*. I learned more about unconditional love, forgiveness, and happiness. Eventually I would free myself from all that negative energy and pain that was built up inside of me. As I completed the lessons in *A Course in Miracles* and continued my spiritual journey, I begin to realize that God loves everybody. He holds nothing against anyone regardless of what they do here on this earth. This was hard to accept at first because I really wanted my husband to be punished for the things that he did. At the end of the day, it's just not how things go, my husband is loved by God just like I am. I went from wanting my husband to be punished to praying for him. During my meditations, I would remain quiet and envision myself along with others having peace and happiness. As I grew spiritually, I came to realize that there is no need for words with God. He already knows what is best for us, so what is the point of asking for things? God will provide us with all we need and more automatically, we don't need to ask. Whether we come to him or not, he knows our thoughts, needs, and desires. Prayer for me is a time to just quiet my mind, letting God know that I love Him, and I want what he wills for me, which is happiness. With happiness and peace, comes everything and more than we can imagine. I learned to want that for myself, my loved ones, strangers and those who I perceived as doing me wrong, my husband included. I went from thoughts of punishment for my husband to wanting nothing but the best for my husband. It didn't matter what the best for him meant either. If his best was loving and being with another woman, that is what I wanted for him. I was healing and came to realize that we all deserve peace and happiness on this earth regardless of our past actions. Somewhere along the way, I was able to visualize my husband's mistress when I meditated. This was a huge step for me and when I began to want good things for her, I knew that I had grown. There was a time when I wanted to choke this woman until her eyeballs popped out of her head. I had a true disliking for this woman and that is me putting it nicely. I let those feelings go, I no longer cared about the nasty things that she did in the past. I was okay with my present and acknowledged that the past no longer existed. If it didn't exist there was no reason to hold on to negative feelings. So, I didn't. Instead I focused on the positive, the here and now. Life was easier after my husband left; it was painful for me, but it was also a huge weight that was lifted off my shoulders. The more happiness and peace that I experienced, the more happiness and peace I wanted for others regardless of the role they played in my life. I switched things up and it felt good. I figured out that forgiveness is not hard and it can be given to anyone for anything regardless of the perceived wrongdoing. Forgiveness is necessary for my own happiness, and I had to be okay with that. I learned to be okay with letting so that I could allow forgiveness to work its magic. Me forgiving my husband and his mistress was necessary for me to move on. It made my process easier and allowed more love to be in my life. I was able to let go of the negative feelings and allowed more room for the positive ones. Similar to that weight that was lifted once my husband was gone, allowing forgiveness felt like more weight being lifted off me. Over time, I was able to switch up my thoughts and it led to a change in my feelings. The results showed in my day-to-day life and happiness was shining off me. Changing the way that I was thinking and feeling helped me a lot. It wasn't about my husband; it wasn't about his mistress. It was about me and my process. If I would have rejected the things that I learned about forgiveness, I would still be full of anger and pain. Instead, I choose to accept what God was showing me and I proceeded accordingly. I trusted the things that I was learning on my spiritual journey, and it worked in my favor. I no longer focused on the negative and claimed the victim. I learned to accept the events that took place and squeezed whatever positive that I could find out of them.

# CHAPTER 9

# This Is Me

When do we really figure ourselves out? Do we know who we are we when come out of the womb, by grade school? Maybe we are constantly trying to figure out who we are for our entire lifetime. How do we know that we know who we are and what happens when we have things figured out? Honestly, I think everyone's journey to find themselves is different. We all take this personal route full of twists and turn until one day there we are, recognizable. If I walked away with anything from the mess that I once called my marriage it would definitely be insight and acceptance. I know myself better than I have ever known myself in my entire life. I also accept what I know about myself and I am unapologetic for it. I have my ways and that's that, take it or leave it. I am far from perfect but at the same time, I know that I am a good and genuine person, willing to share myself with others and offer what I can. The good thing is that I am the best version of myself today and continue to work on myself every day. It feels good to know oneself and can also be more productive.

Knowing myself, I am aware of my triggers, I know my emotions and how to stand behind them versus identify with them. I am in tune with myself and understand myself as I am. I take myself as I am and every day, I love myself for me. I also understand that perfection is not necessary and I do not try to be perfect. I do my best, which is all that I can do and I am okay with this. I was searching for meaning and true happiness before my husband left. After I read the book *Letting Go* I knew that there was more to life than my current awareness. It was at this point that my spiritual journey began. Shortly after, my husband left for the last time and I had the strength to accept this and begin to move on. When he first left, I was left to survive and figure out my next move. As I continued through the process, I began to focus on myself, no longer thinking about my past relationship. I didn't give much thought to my ex at all and when I did have moments, they were brief and less intense. I made it through the survival stage and moved on to finding myself and my purpose. I cannot remember my exact divorce date, but I do remember that by the time the divorce was taking place, I was good. I no longer was afraid of being divorced and I was not worried about anything that had to do with my ex. I do remember that my ex had served me with divorce papers in September 2020. When I received the papers, it didn't even bother me and I was relieved that I would not have to pay for it. Due to Covid 19, it did take some time for us to be seen by a judge but the day came. Thankfully, it was a virtual meeting, so I didn't have to take a lot of time off work and this also meant limited contact with my ex. Of course, he made the whole event more dramatic than necessary but at least it was a virtual setting and no physical contact. During the meeting, my ex had the nerve to request to speak to me privately regarding our relationship and told me that I would always be his wife despite the divorce. I found the whole thing quite amusing, especially since he was the main reason why the divorce was taking place, including the one that filed for the divorce. It is amazing how individuals do not know how to take responsibility for their actions and understand the role they play in situations. It's called accountability and many of us know nothing about the concept. But it truly did not matter, I was in a good place and there was no way that I was going to let this man change that. I allowed him to break me down and destroy me in the past and that was not going to happen ever again. Surviving a traumatic event can change you for the good or the bad. Some people take their trauma and extend it into other people's lives. Treating them the same way that they were treated. Others survive their trauma, moving forward carefully to break the cycle. For myself, I chose to break the cycle. I chose to never put myself in a situation in which love and sincerity are questionable. Because love is not questionable, it is clear and serves one purpose. I also chose to never treat an individual the way I was treated in my marriage. By getting to know myself, I was able to point out my shortcomings and fix them. Being a nicer person became a priority and soon became natural and comfortable. During my marriage, I was so miserable and felt the need to always be on the defense. I had to shake that off and get back to my normal self, which is peaceful and full of love. We all are peaceful and full of love, the issue is that many of us are not aware of this. We each have a part of God in us that has the ability to overshadow any negative characteristic that we may have. We just have to make the decision to identify with our true selves and we will come to realize that love is what we are made of. It is not a hard thing to do but we can make it hard. I have developed my spiritual awareness, yet I continue to struggle with certain things. I am okay with this because I know that I am moving in the right direction. I feel that even a tiny bit of progress is progress. Each step that I take in the right direction is needed to get me where I am going. My experience changed me for the better and I am proud of that. When I was hurt and feeling pain, I choose to turn to God. This was the best decision that I could make because you really can't go wrong relying on him. Today I am better, I am able to talk about past events without any emotion. A few years ago, I would never imagine that I would be this strong. My patience has also grown and I have more control over my temper. There was a time that I would just go off on anyone for anything. Today, I think before I speak, realizing that some battles are just not worth fighting. I understand that everyone is not worth my energy, therefore I stopped being so generous with it. Now when I do have an outburst, which I still do from time to time, I cut them short. I refuse to sit with negative energy for too long. I have learned to offer myself forgiveness for my mistakes as I continue to work on myself. I also forgive others, with no questions asked. Many times, I don't even hold onto anything that is perceived as wrongdoing towards me. I stay away from individuals that trigger me and do not have my best interest in mind. In doing this, I had to cut a few people out of my life. I am okay with this because I have my peace and I will truly take that over any relationship in this world. Matter of fact, I am rather picky with those that I allow to get close to me. I would rather be alone than be around a bunch of people who are not genuine and don't have my best interest in mind. I had to learn through my process that everyone is not like me, we do not all think and move the same. I may be willing to give my honest true self, but that does not mean that the individuals that I encounter are willing or able to do the same. I can only control myself and will never try to change another person. I did that and it drained me to the point where I had absolutely no energy. So, over time I survived, I found myself and became extremely comfortable with the person that I looked at in the mirror. I went into a battle that was unexpected, I never thought that I would have to fight for my husband's love and affection. I came out of the war different, I still have scars but they have healed and I am okay with the mark that was left. I continue to nurse the negative feelings that arise sometimes and I know how to let them pass. I don't think that I will ever be the same, I will never forget that I gave all I had to an individual and it was so unappreciated. But I don't have to let any of that dictate how I will move now or in the future. I know my worth and it is not determined by another individual. I get to decide what I will put up with and how my life will go. For the longest time, I felt low because my ex cheated on me and treated me badly. I gave him any and everything that I could and he chose to give his love to someone else. It really messed up the way I viewed myself for some time. Eventually, I would learn that his actions were not about my worth. I probably had nothing to do with his horrible behavior. A year or so after the divorce, my ex reached out to me through social media. I ignored him because I felt that it was just no point in any communication. He continued to reach out from time to time over the next few months and I continued to ignore him, hoping that he would get the picture. He didn't get the picture, the memo or the email that was sent and therefore continued with his attempts. He would message me that he was sorry, he expressed that he needed to talk to me, he even reminded me of how much time had passed. None of this mattered, I didn't need an apology because forgiveness was already provided. I didn't need a reminder of the time we spent apart, because I was no longer interested. I had no desire to talk because there was nothing left to say. The value that I placed on my ex had decreased a lot and that changed the way I felt about him a lot. Eventually, I gave in and responded to one of his messages. My goal was to get him to stop reaching out but the man was persistent and it didn't quite go that way. We spoke for about a month and saw one another two or three times. It was very uneventful and I constantly questioned what it was that I saw in him in the first place. The interactions were not the same and I truly regretted even answering him. The fact is that I was able to be around him and not bring up the old stuff. I did not have any emotion at all really. It let me know that I truly made it and that was satisfying for me. I was finally over this man and he was completely out of my system. Oh, what a feeling when that person who do you wrong suddenly wants to fix things. I felt good letting him know that there was nothing left to fix and that I just did not feel the same. It wasn't because I wanted him to feel pain, it was because I had gotten over mine.

# CHAPTER 10

# What If

I will never forget one day when I was meditating and particular words popped into my mind. At the time, I was in the beginning stages of meditating, so I was not sure if it was my ego at work or if there was true meaning behind the words. Eventually, I would find out that the words were very meaningful and they popped into my mind for a reason. I would never forget the phrase and to this day I reflect on the words often. I was in the early stages of meditating and I also was experiencing a very important moment in my spiritual journey. I had begun the lessons in *A Course in Miracles* which required me to set aside certain times in the day to sit in a quiet place and reflect on the particular lesson. This is what I was doing when the words popped into my head. I had not mastered quieting that troubling voice in my mind just yet so I had a hard time distinguishing between what I should listen to and what I should not. I started my meditation by repeating the lesson of the day in *A Course in Miracles*. From there, I began to focus on my breathing which allowed that voice in my head to stop talking. I laid there quiet and waiting, for what I am not sure. But I was doing what I felt was needed to grow spiritually and to figure out where I was in my life. After what felt like about five minutes, I sat up. Five minutes for a beginner in meditation can feel like a long time and I had reached my limit. Sitting up with my eyes opened in the quiet room, I began to look around, my mind was still quiet and then I heard these words, "Love yourself as you would love Me. Love others as you would love yourself." Some instances in life cannot be mistaken for anything but God and his love. This is one of those moments, although at that moment, I was a little confused as to who was delivering this message. Deep down I knew it was a message from God and that felt good. It felt good to know that I was close enough to God to hear his voice and receive his message. It felt good that God spoke a message to me which let me know that he was present in my life. Those words stuck with me and continued to stick with me to this day. God is in each one of us, which is why he told me to love others, including myself, the same as I love him. That part of him that is in us, means so much more than any other part of us. For me, it was the piece of him that I have in me that kept me going. When I looked within to find my happiness, I found my true self and it was beautiful. Many times, I think to myself, would I have found this happiness and developed my spirituality if my marriage hadn't been such a failure? I consider the fact that this horrible experience had to take place for me to uncover what was deep inside of me. Would I have read the book *Letting Go* if my husband didn't leave the house and come back talking all this stuff about attachments, which I had no understanding of at the time? If I did not read *Letting Go*, would I have known about *A course in Miracles*, which changed my life and the way I view myself and others? Would I know how to forgive others if I never had to forgive my ex for all things that took place during the marriage? I am not sure if this is where I would be if I didn't have that experience. At the beginning of the breakup, I would often think, "What if..". What if I married this man and he actually knew how to be a man? There would be a different outcome with less pain and suffering. In being a man, my ex would have communicated his feelings, his fears and his insecurities to me. We could have worked them out and supported one another because I had fears and insecurities too. What if I married a man that knew how to love me back and was able to express that love? I probably wouldn't have this fear of relationships and this doubt in a man's ability or willingness to love. I would not have this self-doubt, that I am not able to be loved. The way my ex-husband treated me after giving him the best of me. It left me feeling as if my qualities were worthless, for a long time I couldn't understand what was wrong with me that made him mistreat me. Because for the longest time, I took accountability for his wrongdoings. But what if I didn't, what if I cheated when I first found out that he was cheating? Would he have stayed to work things out, if he knew that I had someone on the side also? What if I left a little sooner or stayed a little longer? It's possible I could have avoided some of the pain I experienced by leaving sooner. Or maybe I would have found out that I was built for much more hurt if I would have stayed a little longer. My ex called me the day after our final breakup, and I choose not to answer the phone. He would not reach out to me again until I was served with divorce papers. What if I answered that phone call, would we have talked it out? Would he have come back home and been a better man? If I am being honest, the answer is hell no. He was not going to change, after all the chances I gave him, he chose to remain the same. I am glad I did not answer that phone call that day. I am glad that I decided to stay strong and move on from the mess that I grew so comfortable with. I am glad that I called out to God to take the pain away and he did just that. I am glad that God spoke to me and helped me to see things differently. As I moved on and lost interest in my ex, I would think about what if I never married him. I passed up some good men for my ex, just to be hurt and disappointed. What if I would have chosen differently, where would I be now in my life? Would I still have my house because I choose a partner that was capable and willing to share the load with me? Would I still be married, celebrating anniversaries and taking wonderful vacations all over the world? Maybe I would have more children because my husband only desired and wanted me. It's possible that my girls would be different because they experienced my ex also. They have emotional scars also, maybe those scars would not be there if I chose differently. If I chose smarter and knew my worth, I would not have married my ex. I have been single since my breakup and sometimes I wonder if I will ever experience a healthy relationship. One that is built on trust, a relationship where I am confident and treated like a queen. A relationship where I do not have to worry about where my man is going when he leaves the house A relationship that does not increase my anxiety, instead it increases my peace. I wonder if I will ever have this, or did I pass up my chance when I chose my ex? What if this marriage was the peak of my love life and if so what the hell did I do wrong in my past life to deserve this? I wish I knew what I know now, I would have made different choices. I wish I was as smart and aware as I am now, my outcome would be different. I look back at the events that took place before the wedding, I look back at the relationship I had with my ex when we were younger. I should have made a better decision. And if I would have done that, how would life be today? I was taught as a little girl to never question God's work. But there is a part of me that would like to know if there could have been a different way. Could I have had a better experience and been able to grow spiritually? Could I have learned about forgiveness another way? I will never know the answer to any of these questions because this is the way my things turned out. At first, I was not okay with the outcome, but as I asked God for peace, I developed the ability to accept this experience and move on. I learned too that I can choose peace rather than focus on the events and outcomes that I didn't want or expect.

Through time I have learned that I learn best through experiences. Unfortunately, I must go through something to fully understand the lesson. From that lesson, I proceed and move accordingly through life. I try not to make the same mistake twice especially when it comes to dealing with others. Let's just say, I live by the saying "Fool me once shame on you, fool me twice shame on me". I am not going to let someone continue to keep playing with me. Once my eyes are open, I have a clear plan and become determined, I am done. If I had to give anyone advice, it would be that two things are necessary to make changes in life. First, there must be an awareness that there is an issue. Second, there needs to be motivation to take action to fix the issue. It took me a very long time to become aware and accept my awareness of my marriage. Thankfully, it didn't take me long to develop the motivation to take action. Once I had a clear idea that my ex did not love me the way I thought, I took action. I remained motivated and despite all the fears that I had, I made up my mind and refused to look back regardless of how uncomfortable it became. The beginning was the worst and that is when I did the smartest thing I could, I relied on God. It was all I could do and it was all that I needed to do. There was a time that I could not think of my ex or his mistress without experiencing a negative emotion. My heart rate would increase and I would break out in tears at the thought that my ex loved another woman more than me. I could sit in misery all day thinking about this man and all the stuff that we went through. Today it is not possible for me to shed a tear over any of that. Not only do I refuse to think about these individuals but I truly have also so much more that I would rather think about. Days, weeks, and months go by and I do not think about my ex at all, and when I do think of him no emotions follow. I no longer place value on him our past relationship, or any of the things that he has done. The past is gone and no longer exists. I am safe in the present and I have peace. My future is bright, and I am not worried because my ex has no access to me. I am stronger and I know my worth, so he can never hurt me again, I would never allow that. Yet the question remains what if I didn't experience any of this? What could I have done to avoid this man, this marriage and this experience? There are even times when I wonder how life would be if I had a chance to warn my younger self about life. If I could talk to my younger self, would I even give a warning? Or would I choose to just provide her with advice to help her face the challenges in her future life? What if I could talk to my younger self, what would I say to that beautiful young girl who loves to read books? That young girl who is a bit shy and never quite fits in with any groups at school. The young girl who fantasized about having the family that she never had. What would I say to that little girl if I could talk to her now? If I could talk to her, would she even listen? I am not sure but if I could talk to my younger self, this is what I would say:

*First, I want to let you know that no matter what, please know you are loved. Life is going to be full of ups and downs, but you will conquer all. Learn to be uncomfortable and take more chances. Fear belongs nowhere near your heart, yet it is something that you will struggle with throughout life. But don't worry, you will overcome. Do not settle, instead reach for the stars because they are within your grasp and you are deserving of the best. With that being said, there will be many times in which you will take way less than what you deserve. You are a giver, a care-taker, you are smart and genuine. You will learn from your experiences but the process will include disappointment and pain. Don't worry though, you will make it and you will be okay. Have no regrets and just know that it is what it is. It's easier to accept the situation and adjust than it is to fight the evitable. Most of all be confident in yourself and stand up for what you believe in. Love others regardless of how they treat you and practice forgiveness because you are going to need it. Stay close to God and know that His will is for you to be happy. Understand that life is all about perception- the way you view a situation will dictate the way in which you react. Think positive and be a leader. Please know that everything will be okay. Look for happiness from within, that is where you will find it along with peace. Know that you are loved and that is all you need to be.*

I would hug my younger self kiss her and reassure her that she is going to grow into a wonderful woman. There is nothing that we can do to prepare ourselves for life. It just doesn't work out that way, we can plan and take steps, thinking that we are preparing. But life happens and there are always things that we cannot see or imagine happening in our future. Life will present us with experiences that we do not know how to plan for. Life will not stop and wait for us to adjust; it keeps on going with the expectation that we will continue on. Typically, we do because as humans we have survival instincts that allows us to keep up with life and all its twists and turns. We also have God, who is always with us, He never leaves us. He is always willing to assist, we just need to ask and trust in him to get us through. From this experience, I learned that God loves me and with him I can do anything, including getting over disappointment and heartbreak. I am no longer broken and I never was because I can only be love, which is constant and forever unchanging.

Looking back on the past few years, I am very thankful that I made it. I allowed myself to suffer and I lost myself trying to fit into another person's life. I learned a lot about myself and I have a clear vision of where I am going. One thing for sure is that I would rather be alone and happy than be in a relationship and be miserable. I know where happiness comes from and it is from within. External things come and go, making the happiness that they bring temporary. I understand that I can choose happiness regardless of any circumstance that I face. This is because I have an endless reservoir of love right inside of me. For the longest time, I wanted to write a book. I have always been a reader since a young girl. Ever since I could remember, I thought of writing and creating something special. Fear kept me in my marriage despite the events that took place time after time. Fear also arose at the thought of writing about this experience or writing about anything for that matter. I had to let that fear go to move on from my breakup and I let it go again when I decided to sit down and start writing. As I began to write, I let go of more and more fear. As I wrote, I felt lighter and better. The more words that I typed, the more positive energy consumed me. I am so thankful for the people that are in my life that encouraged me to write. Years ago, I would not even tell a soul that I was interested in writing. One day I mentioned it to a close friend and his feedback was everything. He simply told me, "Of course you can do it!" Hearing someone tell me that I could do something that I was so fearful of doing, gave me confidence. I began to talk about writing to a few other people that were close to me and continued to get the same reaction, they would tell me yes, "Write a book!" It would still take me some time before I actually opened the laptop and got to it but the words from my loved ones remained in my mind. I don't even remember what prompted me to actually start writing, but one day I just did it. Writing for me was refreshing, I had to recall memories that were once painful. But as I wrote about them, I felt nothing and that let me know that I was okay. I choose to write about my marriage and the things that I went through because they made me who I am today. Although there were so many moments that I felt broken and like I was losing. But the truth is that I survived and I was given the opportunity to piece myself back together again. I am better than ever and thankful for my experiences, the good and the bad. For some reason, I needed that experience to be a part of my journey to get me where I am going. I no longer question it because I am at peace with the situation. I accepted it as part of my story and hope that my experience may impact others. As I wrote my story, I constantly kept in mind my intentions. I didn't use names because I did not intend to paint a negative picture of anyone involved. I told my story as I perceived it and based on my experiences. It was about me and my process with nothing to do with anyone else. I didn't see the point in using names or providing information that would single out anyone or possibly do harm to anyone in any way. I wrote to express myself and to completely close a chapter in my life that no longer deserves any of my attention or energy. I wrote to prove to myself that I am okay. I am more than okay; I am resilient, and I am loved. I wrote with the hopes that one person would read about my experience and realize that they too are loved. Despite any external circumstances, happiness is always an option, we just have to choose it. I hope that my story can help others who may be facing hard times. I hope that they can read this and have a clear understanding that they too can overcome. Anything is possible with God, and he is always present. Everything that we experience in life serves a purpose. Every experience has a positive aspect, it's all about perception. If you cannot find the positive in the experience, just change your perception. The positive is there, waiting to be exposed.

# Bibliography


Dr. Schucman, Helen. (1975). *A Course in Miracles*. Huntington Station, New York: Foundation for Inner Peace.

Hawkins, D.R. (2018). *Letting Go: The Pathway of Surrende*r. Hay House Inc, Carlsbad, CA.

Ruiz, D.M. (1997). *The Four Agreements: A Practical Guide to Personal Freedom.* Amber-Allen Publishing, San Rafael, CA.

Walsch, N.D. (1995). Conversations with God, An Uncommon Dialogue. Book 1. Hampton Roads Publishing Company, Inc, Charlottesville, VA.